W0259422

ADOLF LOOS
A PRIVATE PORTRAIT

ADOLF LOOS

A Private Portrait

BY

CLAIRE BECK LOOS

EDITED BY

CARRIE PATERSON

DoppelHouse Press | Los Angeles, California

FRONTISPIECE | Adolf Loos in his Vienna apartment where he lived with Claire Beck Loos, Giselastrasse 3 (now Bösendorferstrasse), Vienna I. Apartment interior is now in the Historical Museum of Vienna.
PHOTOGRAPH: Claire Beck.

SET IN CASLON & FUTURA | DESIGNED BY CURT CARPENTER
FIRST EDITION

ISBN 978-0-9832540-0-3

DoppelHouse Press | Los Angeles, California

PRINTED IN THE UNITED STATES OF AMERICA

CONTENTS

ACKNOWLEDGEMENTS

Adolf Loos — A Private Portrait is the first English translation of Claire Beck Loos' 1936 book *Adolf Loos Privat.* Constance C. Pontasch artfully achieved its first iteration in the 1990s. In 2010 *Adolf Loos — A Private Portrait* benefitted from literary and linguistic advice contributed by Nicholas Saunders. To both of them great credit is due for their careful and intelligent responses to the nuances of Claire Beck Loos' text.

The supplemental documents to *Adolf Loos — A Private Portrait* were compiled through the efforts of Claire Beck Loos' niece and nephew Janet Beck Wilson and Charles Paterson (Karl Schanzer), with Charles' wife Fonda Paterson, and their daughter Carrie Paterson. They have been edited in part by Hensley Peterson, Nicholas Saunders, and book designer Curt Carpenter. Linda Engle, Mark Addison, and Beatrice Lang have contributed valuable clarifications and offered discerning advice. The Beck and Paterson families consider all of these people fellow travellers on their journey to catch glimmers of those truths lost in time, and thank them gratefully.

A key to Claire's discreet shorthand for names of people referenced in her book has been reprinted from Adolf Opel's 1985 edition of *Adolf Loos Privat.* Opel is a tireless researcher and has continually and generously encouraged the Beck descendants to keep Claire Beck Loos' work in the public sphere. Many thanks are due him.

Until the early 1990's, the full content of *Adolf Loos Privat* and other documented details of Claire's life were a mystery to the surviving generations of the Beck family, who never spoke, or don't now, speak German. To read and translate documents and books for the publication of *Adolf Loos — A Private Portrait* they have worked appreciatively with Gunar Hochheiden, Doris Berger, and Sina Rahmani. Many thanks are extended to Janet Wilson and Fonda Paterson for their persistent efforts to research and record family history, and to Will Casey for scanning delicate hand-written letters with Nazi censure stamps. Fonda enlisted the help of Constance C. Pontasch to translate these documents, which had carefully been filed and stored by Claire's brother-in-law Steve Shanzer (Stefan Schanzer), the original addressee, but which up until April of 2010 had been left unread by anyone except him. Other letters presumably sent by Claire to her brother Max Beck no longer exist, for painful reasons that were known and borne by Max alone.

Constance's initial translation of *Adolf Loos Privat,* which Fonda arranged as a present for her husband Charles and the other Beck descendants — Doris Schneider and family, Janet Wilson and her mother Elizabeth Beck —, had been kept in the family until recently, when the resurgence of interest in Adolf Loos encouraged the family to republish the book in English.

Key supporters in this endeavor have been Hensley Peterson, who has been devoted to Claire like a member of her

own family, and the Czech architect, historian and writer Ivan Margolius. Ivan is the author of *Reflections of Prague: Journeys through the 20th Century* and other works, and son of the late Heda Margolius Kovály, author of the book *Under a Cruel Star: A Life in Prague 1941–1968,* among others. In nothing less than a haunting coincidence, Ivan's paternal grandparents were on the same transport from Terezín to Riga as Claire in 1942. Seeing "Loosova, Klara Franziska" on the list for transport "P" while researching his own family, effectively brought Ivan and the Beck descendants together. After discussing the English translation with Janet, he suggested the book be put forward into public view to benefit a wider audience of Loos scholars.

As a family, we are pleased to present *Adolf Loos — A Private Portrait* to the English-speaking world on the occasion of the exhibition *Learning to Dwell: Adolf Loos in the Czech Lands*, organized by Maria Szadkowska, curator at Loos' Villa Müller, and by the City of Prague Museum, for the Royal Institute of British Architecture. We thank Maria for her help and kindness, and for providing the picture with Loos and Claire from Loos' 60th birthday party.

Only one thousand copies of this English edition have been printed, the same number of copies as Claire published of *Adolf Loos Privat* in 1936. We reach back to her time to honor her memory with this gesture.

BIOGRAPHY OF ADOLF LOOS

Adolf Loos (December 10, 1870–August 23, 1933) was born in Brno, in what is now the Czech Republic. Son of a stonemason and sculptor, Loos studied architecture in Dresden between 1890-1893. He lived in the United States for three years following his education and then moved to Vienna to practice architecture in 1896. Within Vienna's lively *fin de siècle* café culture he began to formulate his ideas on cultural reform and urban development, beginning what was virtually a second career as a writer and lecturer. Primarily he published articles in the *Neue Freie Presse*, but also briefly put out his own publication, *Das Andere [The Other]*, which was a journal promoting "the introduction of Western Civilization into Austria." Loos' writings were later collected in several volumes, including *Ins Leere Gesprochen [Spoken into the Void]* in 1921, and *Trotzdem [Nevertheless]* in 1931.

Loos was influenced both by the Greek architect Vetruvius and Anglophone culture, and incorporated aspects of classical architecture into his early work. Of these, a notable design was for the Chicago Tribune Tower (1922, un-built), a skyscraper in the form of a Greek column. Loos' use of iconography in this manner was short-lived, as he turned his attention to revolutionizing building practices, valorizing the craftsman and the laborer, opposing the "wasteful" ornamentation of the Viennese Secession, and pioneering the use of raw materials for their simplicity and beauty.

In Loos' radical public projects like the Goldman & Salatsch building (1909–1911) on Michaelerplatz in Vienna, the defining distinction between façade and interior in Loos' architecture can still be observed. Among Vienna's other architectural attractions are Loos' Café Museum (1899), The American Bar (Kärntnerbar, 1907), and Knize Men's Outfitters (1909–1913).

During his lifetime Loos designed, built, and remodelled close to one hundred apartments and homes, and undertook a number of large civic projects like schools, government buildings, and workers' housing. Dozens of additional works included sanatoriums, hotels, cafés and bars, and shops. Several of Loos' projects were not realized but still remain influential, like the black-and-white striped marble house for Josephine Baker (1928) with its dramatic lighting and view underwater into the swimming pool.

Most relevant to this book perhaps, Loos created stunning interiors using marble and wood veneers, and was known for his generous living spaces. His development of the *Raumplan* — open-space architecture conceived in three-dimensions — can be seen in notable homes like the Villa Müller (1928–30) in Prague, Czech Republic, now a museum and considered one of Loos' most important contributions to Modern architecture. After more than a century, people continue to rediscover the brilliance and forethought of this architectural master.

INTRODUCTION

Claire Beck Loos was the last wife of the Czechoslovak-Viennese architect and cultural critic Adolf Loos, and one of the first to memorialize him in a book, which was intended to raise money for a fitting tombstone to mark Loos' gravesite. *Adolf Loos Privat* was published in 1936 and is printed here for the first time in English as *Adolf Loos — A Private Portrait.* It is a small jewel of literature, a portrait of a man and mentor, as seen by his young wife, caretaker, interpreter, secretary, and often proxy, as he descended into deafness and skirted the edge of death.

In the Loos archives at the Albertina in Vienna, correspondence from the 1930's between Claire and the Loos expert Dr. Ludwig Münz document the lengths the Beck family, and particularly Claire, went to in order to raise funds for Loos' self-specified grave marker. When funds from initial book sales were not enough, Claire solicited Loos' friends and admirers for the remaining balance, calling on those like Loos' former student Kurt Unger (as Claire once wrote, "Loos' warrior") who had provided for Loos when he was alive. Whether she succeeded or not in this endeavour is still unclear.

Adolf Loos passed away on August 23, 1933, destitute, from long-standing health complications at a nursing home in Kalksburg. He left behind the strong echo of his voice in his writings and within the echo chambers of his architecture, his influential presence. During Loos' particularly serious bout of illness in 1931 Claire recorded his designs for an *Ehrengrab*, literally a "grave of honor." In 1934 he was conferred one when his body was moved to the Zentralfriedhof to rest amongst Vienna's finest writers, composers, and cultural icons; but it was not until 1956, however, that the grey granite block he had specified would be installed. After Loos died, it seems that Claire imagined this short book as an additional memorial, which could substitute for the architectural monument he desired.

Through Claire it is possible to hear a more intimate Loos than the one recorded by experts, historians, and by his own hand. During Claire and Loos' time together she heard his affection, his scorn, his aphorisms and stories, and transcribed his dictations, which bordered on histrionics when he was ill. With his manner of speaking quite clearly ingrained, Claire Beck Loos leaves the reader with a sense of living with the man, in the environment of his unique psychological architecture.

Claire's private portrait also makes it possible to hear some semblance of the way Loos talked — to friends, clients, wives, students, craftsmen, artists, and society. One can read in Claire's work a mirroring of the last collection of Loos' writings, *Trotzdem*, published in 1931; her similar spare style of vignette vividly reenacts his personality through imagistic narrative and dialogue. One also notices that she created the text in homage to Loos' own aphoristic style. While her memory of him is flattering at times, it is not at others; he could be a tyrant as much as he was a vibrant genius. But regardless, hers is a welcome and humanizing counter-balance to the reification of "the great God Loos" as he was called, which proceeded gradually during his life, and hastened after his death. Claire's small volume provides the reader an opportunity to be in conversation with Loos the man and the architect.

As noted by editor Adolf Opel in his introduction to the 1985 edition of *Adolf Loos Privat,* the first public recognition for Claire's book came in 1935, when the *Neue Freie Presse* published excerpts on the second anniversary of Loos' death. The newspaper praised *Adolf Loos Privat* as "valuable" and "a *document humain,*" and composer Ernst Krenek wrote an article therein that described Claire's writing aptly as "snapshots." She was, after all, trained in photography and worked professionally in the atelier of Hede Pollak in Prague. Though Claire took many images of Loos herself, she chose to use Pollak's famous portrait of him on the original book cover. In this English language edition, Claire's own portrait of Loos reading in the inglenook of his Vienna flat, where they lived together, has been used instead.

It has recently come to light that during Claire's two difficult years in Prague between 1940 and 1941, she had a job as an unpaid assistant for another photographer. This fact is known through letters from Claire and her mother Olga Beck, which have been preserved since the war years by Claire's sister Eva's family. By working for this photographer, who is not named, Claire could experiment with a Leica camera, which Olga mentions Claire would not be able to take with her if they succeeded in getting emigration papers to Cuba or Ecuador. Also mentioned is that the photographer was making images in the style of the *Bewegung*, an art movement that had influenced Loos.

Claire was most likely exposed to the *Bewegung* art movement during her years of artistic experimentation in Paris, even before she began a relationship with the architect. While very little of Claire's photographic record is known to remain, here in *Adolf Loos — A Private Portrait*, select images taken by Claire have been included in the Appendix. Among these are portraits of Loos with Claire's family and friends, as well as what may have been a self-portrait taken toward the end of her life.

Claire (Klara) Beck was born on November 4, 1904 in Pilsen, Czechoslovakia, the middle child of Olga and Otto Beck, secular Jews whose families had lived for generations in the Czech lands, at the heart of the Austro-Hungarian Empire. They were industrialists; Otto Beck was a partner with Wilhelm and Richard Hirsch in a Pilsen wire manufacturing company, and Olga Beck came from a hops and brewing family. Wilhelm Hirsch, Otto's first cousin, was also one of Loos' first clients, as were other members of the extended family by marriage like Alfred Kraus, who married Wilhelm's sister Rosa; and Gustav and Marie (Kraus) Turnowsky. Also, Oskar and Hanne Semler, close family friends of the Becks, hired Loos to do several remodelling projects.

Claire and Loos met each other when she was a teenager. He had designed the Beck family's first flat near the Pilsen Opera House in 1908, which was modified and re-installed in another building overlooking the large park on Benešplatz (now Náměstí Míru) in 1928. As Claire relates, her father had first been interested in Loos through his writings published in the *Neue Freie Presse* and followed the architect's career with great interest.

In 1929, Claire and Loos met again in the Bohemian circles she was then a part of in Paris. They mixed together in the cafés with writers and artists, perhaps even clients like Dadaist Tristan Tzara for whom Loos had already completed a house. The couple became engaged after seeing a Josephine Baker performance in Vienna to which Loos had invited the Beck family. Her parents at first protested the arrangement; they considered Loos, at thirty-four years her senior, to be much too old for her, and in too poor health to be a suitable husband.[1] In spite of her family's opposition, Claire married Loos in Vienna on July 18, 1929, when she was twenty-four. The Jewish rabbinical authorities refused to validate a mixed marriage, and ultimately, Otto Beck did not attend the wedding.

Loos and Claire were divorced on April 30, 1932. It is clear from a letter Loos wrote to his student Kurt Unger on October 29, 1931 that he and Claire had already separated by this time; in the brief missive Loos recounted rumors of

1 Translations of letters documenting this time are included in the photo appendix.

Claire being romantically involved with others, one named simply as "Bauer." By January 1932 Claire had requested formal divorce papers through Dr. Gustav Scheu — another client of Loos in Vienna — relinquishing any rights to alimony, with her parents both in agreement not to press Loos for any compensation, as long as he admitted responsibility.

Claire's retrospective memoir captures the personal and social transformative power of Loos' work, but within the contradictions of the man. On July 4, 1929, Loos wrote to Claire that he liked the Jews "better than people from Vienna," barely a compliment. Separately, with some irony, he called himself an "anti-Semite" but made no secret of having had several Jewish wives. A short chapter reveals Claire's emphasis on such statements and lays bare Loos' internal logic, which at the same time places him within larger trends toward anti-Semitism already apparent in the 1930's and felt by her extended family. In her book, Claire shows these insidious effects through a literary analogy of the photographic process of self-portraiture. She writes in a manner that recalls her photographer contemporaries like Ilse Bing, who famously captured herself by mirror as both author and subject of a portrait. The reader will notice that in certain moments Claire flips between the first and third person, as if she is both inhabiting a frame, and at the same time watching herself like a character in it. This dissociative process may reflect her outsider status, a feeling of abjectness, and of being an object in a larger social narrative. Nevertheless, she portrays herself always redeemed in the eyes of Loos.

Adolf Loos — A Private Portrait distinguishes itself in its literary experimentation, and its use of language. Much like a work of modern architecture, it uses an efficient, precise, and spare vocabulary, with little ornamentation. This aspect is noticeable in the English version, but it is even more pronounced in the German, where word-concepts tend to accumulate like long strings, or train carriages. Claire has deliberately chosen words that are direct, clean, and punctuate space with a consistent measure, as if she were parsing her phrases to Loos himself, a nearly deaf man who could still hear, through her. Perhaps her first vignette is even an indication for the reader of the approach one might take with the book — that it could be read out loud — and thus Claire's stories about Loos might be enjoyed much as his own writings were in the coffeehouses, in dialogue with other people.

Claire, like Loos, had a wonderful sense of humor, and the book is filled with moments of comedic timing. Part performance, part memorial, Claire has truly brought her own voice, and Loos' alive. Cues from Loos' letters fill out these impressions. During their courtship, Loos wrote to Claire about missing her "sweet saxophone voice" (April 8, 1929). Indeed the narrative moments in Claire's text are melodic and rich, and Loos helps recall something about her that none of us alive now can even know — her sensuous, resonant way of speaking. One might transpose this effect throughout the text from one of her stories where she sings Schönberg's *Gurrelieder* into

Loos' ear horn, and he asks her to sing it for him again, to sing it all day long.

Loos also admired and was encouraging of Claire's writing. As documented in *Adolf Loos — Leben und Werk*, on July 4, 1929 he wrote to her that he just finished a novel in the newspaper and was imagining she could have written it. When she agrees to marry him, she engenders the following response from him, translated into English by Gunar Hochheiden. On June 25, 1929: "My dear Lerle, what a beautiful letter I have received from you! I would like to publish it to the whole world; all the people should participate in my happiness. Nobody will believe what a nice wife I will get. The letter is a great poem in prose. ... Thousands of kisses everywhere, your husband Dolf." The content of what she expressed to him in her letters may remain however, unfortunately for us, a mystery.

What Claire imparts in her unofficial biography will be important to those just learning about Loos as much as those with a keen interest. But in addition to an understanding of the man, Claire's vignettes are also a self-portrait of the young woman, a writer and photographer, who loved Loos and died prematurely, before her own artistic vision was completely set forth through a full lifetime of work. One can only wonder what the impact he evidently made upon her would have resulted in, had she lived beyond the war.

CARRIE PATERSON

ADOLF LOOS
A PRIVATE PORTRAIT

FOREWORD

I have written this book from memory. I have tried to portray Adolf Loos in a form that will hopefully give the reader an understanding of his strong personality. I am aware of the shortcomings that are inherent to this kind of reporting, but have chosen to write this way, as it seemed important to me to preserve in the material the vitality that came from living together with Loos. Should errors in my recollections, which I can no longer verify today, have crept in then I ask that they be forgiven, considering what I have said above. Remaining plans, notes, drawings and letters will be compiled in other books by experts; my book should therefore not be viewed as a reference book but instead simply as a remembrance of my life with Adolf Loos.

I am dedicating the royalties from this book as a contribution towards establishing Loos' tomb.

CLAIRE LOOS.

HOW IT ALL CAME ABOUT

A stranger asks my father: "How did you make the acquaintance of Loos? How did you get to have Loos do your interior remodel?"

Father tells him: "I lived as a young man in a small provincial Austrian city. At the time, Adolf Loos' essays were being published in the *Neue Freie Presse.* I was only a very low ranking employee and did not have the money to subscribe to the newspaper. So I looked for it at the coffee house and read it there because I found Loos' articles very interesting. But a lot of people were in the same situation I was. There was always fighting over the newspaper and it was always gone. During one such dispute, a patron just decided to jump up on a table and began reading the article out loud.

And that is what they did from then on. In those days the coffee house seemed to be more like a meeting place, and afterwards there would be a lot of discussion.

It was my greatest desire to have Loos do my interior remodel someday ... But it was many years until that would happen ..."

THIS PICTURE HAS GOT TO GO

I am fifteen years old. I go into the big living room to get a book. Two men are there. One of them is Professor L., the other one I do not know. The stranger kneels halfway down onto the bench seat and removes a picture from the wall. He is wearing a brown suit and a cream-coloured shirt. His face is slender and youthful.

"I would just like to know," he says, "who painted this trash. This picture has got to go."

I say: "I painted this picture, and it was for my father's birthday!"

"Well, well," says the stranger, "for your father's birthday, that is of course another matter." Almost tenderly, he hangs the picture back up on the wall. "So you must be the daughter of the owner?"

"And you," I ask inquisitively, "who then are you?"

The stranger looks at me, smiling: "I am Adolf Loos!"

JOSEPHINE BAKER DANCES IN VIENNA

Josephine Baker is dancing in Vienna.

Loos, who has a business meeting with my father, invites all of us to the Varieté where Josephine Baker is dancing. Sitting beside the beautiful, intelligent Frau X. he looks eagerly at the stage and says: "Did you know that Josephine counts me among the best Charleston dancers in Paris?"

"That is certainly a compliment, dear Loos," says the beautiful woman, smiling.

"I have even earned money by dancing," Loos says proudly.

"Money by dancing?" Frau X. asks slowly, raising her eyebrows. "You really must tell us about that," she adds, amused.

Loos looks at Frau X. with an expression of pure, unadulterated joy. "It was quite simple: at an elegant bar, I asked a stranger to a dance. After the dance, she pressed a large coin into my hand."

"And you took the money?" asks Frau X., truly shocked.

Loos looks astonished at the dismayed expression on her face. "But of course. I have never been as proud of any money I earned as I was of that. Just think how well I must have danced and how wonderful I must have looked for her to have thought I was employed as a dancer there! But then, I had a perfect instructor: Josephine Baker! ––– Long live Josephine," Loos cries out loudly and applauds. Josephine appears, dressed in a few green feathers, and gracefully curtsies to all sides. “She did not recognize me,” Loos says, hurt, “or else she definitely would have come over to our table.”

Josephine dances. Loos watches her attentively. “I consider Josephine to be a very great artist,” he says softly. “Just look at what grace and what strength there is in her movements. She always reminds me of an animal in the wild. But the people here have no understanding of her great art,” he adds sadly. “They only see her beautiful body. In Paris it is quite different. There the whole house cheers with enthusiasm when Josephine dances.” Loos falls silent. When Josephine finishes, he applauds with all his might, spurring the rest of the audience again and again to new roaring ovations.

Josephine now selects a partner from the audience. Amid general laughter, a good-natured elderly gentleman gets up on stage. “This number,” Loos says, “was a huge success for Josephine in Prague. She had chosen a thin, agile man from the audience. It was none other than Vlasta Burian, the greatest Czech comedian. It would be impossible to describe her growing astonishment as Burian did the most amazing capers, for she was completely unaware who he was. The audience was screaming with laughter. But Josephine kept animating him to do new tricks.” Loos laughs softly.

“Yes, Josephine is unique … Still, recently I did get upset with her. It was in Paris. She came to me and was in a bad mood. Just think, Loos, she pouted, I want to do big, big remodelling in my house and do not like plans of architects. I was beside myself. What, you did not come to me first? Don't you know that I can design the most beautiful plan in the world for you? Josephine stares at me with her childlike eyes and slowly asks: You are an architect??? – She had no idea who I was. – I drew up a plan for Josephine … I consider it one of my best. The exterior wall is covered with white and black marble slabs – diagonally striped. The most beautiful thing in the house is the bathroom – with its ethereal lighting…" Just at that moment a red rose comes flying onto our table. Josephine has discovered Loos. With a graceful leap she is now at our table herself. "Loos," she calls, "dear Loos, I'm so happy that you here," and with that she stretches out both hands to him. The great man blushes like a little boy.

After the performance, Loos says to me in a low voice so our companion cannot hear him: "Why don't you call me sometime? My number is in the telephone book. We could go out once by ourselves."

It seems incomprehensible to me that Loos can be reached by telephone like any other mortal ---

KÄRNTNERBAR

I meet Loos in front of the opera. We stroll along the Kärntnerstrasse. We stop in front of a bookstore and Loos draws my attention to a simple book cover that appeals to him. Right after that, he discovers in a display a cigarette case of light poplar. He decides to use poplar wood as paneling in a dining room in P. We turn into a side street and go into an elegant little bar. While we are sipping orangeade sitting on the high stools at the bar, Loos says: "I decorated this bar many years ago. It was the first American bar in Vienna. It was originally only thought of for men. The women were quite up in arms about that. Everyday it was packed and the bar overcrowded, but all women were turned away. Countesses and princesses would lead the way, they would beg and they would threaten, but it was no use. They were not allowed in. Public curiosity grew day by day. It was causing quite a sensation in all of Vienna and gave the bar a lot of free advertising. Finally, after five weeks, the situation became intolerable. The women forced their way in."

Loos points at the ceiling: "These marble panels caused a lot of trouble. The Italian specialist who had been working on them suddenly refused to put up the ceiling. He said: 'It will definitely fall down.' I answered: 'Put it up anyway.' The Italian became furious and threw himself at me. The very next minute he was ashamed of his conduct. He asked me for forgiveness and, filled with remorse, asked: 'How can I make up for this?' I answered calmly: 'Put up the ceiling.' It has to this day, after more than twenty years, not fallen down."

THINK IT OVER WELL

Loos is lying stretched out on a corner bench in the dining room asleep. Kulka, the architect, is sitting at the table with a worried look on his face. In front of him is a pile of letters and cards. He looks up for a moment as I come in, then points discontented to the mail. "Nothing but unanswered letters," he sighs. "And then the master is surprised when he loses projects." I sit down quietly at the table. "You know, in the past I always used to do that work," he continues, "but now I have my own business. There is not enough time. The poor master cannot do everything himself either. And then there are always people distracting him from his work." Kulka looks over to the sleeping man with a gently reproachful look. I immerse myself in thought, moved by his words. Kulka is right. Adolf Loos, the great man, gives away his heart, his strength to everybody who comes to him for help. But who helps him? And then, as if Kulka had read my thoughts, he says: "No one helps him. Everyone just comes to him for help. Couldn't you take care of a little of this abandoned mail? Adolf Loos needs someone." "Do you think, Herr Kulka," I ask timidly, "that I can really help him?"

Kulka, the architect, looks at me with a friendly expression: "Give it a try."

I sort the mail into a letter file, which Kulka has quickly supplied. Suddenly Loos awakens. He sits up, yawns, clears his throat, clears his throat more loudly as if to assure himself he is not dreaming … There is a look of total astonishment on his face. Suddenly, he joyously exclaims: "Would you like to always stay with me and work with me? Until now, I have always worked for my women and have tried to make them great and famous, as actresses, dancers. What for? What for? Maybe they would've been happier to remain with me and darn socks." Loos falls silent, gazes off into space. Suddenly, his face brightens. He stands up, takes both of my hands: "But you, you will become no actress, no dancer. You will work with me. It is not easy. Think it over well. My life is a chain of disappointments …"

LOOS HELPS OUT

I am invited to dine at Loos'. Apart from me, there is another guest present, R. P., a young writer. Loos had not even known him before. A few things he read from him pleased him very much. He invited him. As the young artist describes to Loos his difficult situation – he has a family to support –, Loos is very touched. He promises to help. "In Vienna I can do little for you. Go to Berlin. I have good friends there, I will give you some recommendations." Without asking the young man any further, Loos buys him a ticket to Berlin.

A few weeks later a letter arrives from Berlin:

19. March 1929.

Dear Herr Loos!

Myself, my wife, and my child send you our sincere, and best regards. Things will start moving ahead here; it is just a little hard in the beginning with a family. Starting on April 1 however, I will have a steady job. I just have to hang on until then. I hope that you are in good health.

Your ever-thankful
R. P.

"Hang on," says Loos, "with what?" And so he calls up a wealthy client: "Please send some money to R. P. immediately."

ON THE LAURENZIBERG

We are in Prague. We are walking up the Laurenziberg. It is spring and everything is in bloom. Loos speaks:

"On top of the Laurenziberg I would like to build a hotel; it would fit in well with the landscape. A second Kobenzl ... Just think, the Hradshin, this magnificent view and as its complement the Laurenziberg with a hotel that can be seen from far away! I have a plan in mind ... a wonderful plan! The cable railway would have to be put back into operation again; visitors from all over the world would stay there. Something like that is missing in Prague!"

Chatting along like this, we have reached the top of the Laurenziberg. There is a little measly tavern. We order two glasses of curdled milk. The innkeeper, a fat woman with an unfriendly face, sets them in front of us without a word. Dusk is starting to fall.

"In the evening," Loos continues to fantasize, "when Prague is shining with the sparkle of lights, what a view the lucky residents of the hotel would enjoy!" Loos stares contemplatively into the distance. "Oh, Lerle, how happy I would be if I could build that hotel," he says humbly, "How nice would that be ...!" Suddenly: "I left my wallet behind in the hotel. Do you have any money with you?" I have none. "I don't even have my watch with me."

We look at each other without word. Both of us are thinking of the mean face of the innkeeper. "Come on then,"

I murmur. Silently we take each other's hands … we will come back sometime soon and pay. Hand in hand, we walk down the mountain. The path seems endless. What will the innkeeper say when she finds the abandoned glasses we barely touched?!

SHIMMERING FISH

The construction of the Müller house is still in the very early stages. Dr. Müller has taken Loos to the construction site for a meeting. Loos stands between some beams and points to a location. "Here," he says, "is where the illuminated aquarium with the fish will be." No one understands him. The client wants to move on – there are so many important things to discuss. But Loos remains still, unconcerned, and continues: "This will be the favorite place of the master of the house; when he comes home in the evening tired from work, he will watch the fish silently playing. In the light of the lamps they will shimmer in all colours." The client is already getting very annoyed, but Loos does not let it bother him. He – the only one who does not see the boards and scaffolds but rather the finished house – talks today only of the shimmering fish.

SCHÖNBERG'S GURRELIEDER IS PERFORMED IN VIENNA...

Loos recounts: "I can remember the premiere performance as if it were yesterday! Not one ticket had been sold by noon. On the spur of the moment, I took the last of my money and bought up the entire concert hall. Then I stood on the Kärntnerstrasse and handed out tickets to acquaintances and strangers – whoever came my way. That evening the hall was packed full. Some friends and I had scattered ourselves throughout the entire concert hall so that we could intervene in the event of an uproar. My wife Bessie was in the gallery.

"Sure enough, hissing and grumbling did break out after the first movement. My wife threw herself like a beast at the disrupters and began walloping them ... Yes, Bessie was quite a character!" Loos falls wistfully silent. (Bessie had died of pulmonary disease).

"Have you ever heard the Gurrelieder?" I answer no. "Oh, Lerle, what a shame, I know them by heart!" Losing himself in thought, he begins to hum to himself, then sings out, purely and clearly, a main motif. Suddenly he turns silent, his eyes open wide, contorting with fear. "Lerle, Lerle, do you hear me?" Thinking back, he has forgotten his deafness. "Lerle, I can't hear anymore, I am completely deaf!" He claps both hands in front of his face with a painful, lamenting cry; then, quietly straightening up, he begins to sing again – this time very loudly, with wide-opened eyes. I grab the ear horn and hand it to him. Hesitating, he puts it up to his ear and looks at me with questioning, anxious eyes. As loudly as I can, I repeat the motif into the ear horn.

"Not so loud, I am not deaf you know," he shouts delighted. A smile moves over his face, coming to rest in his golden brown eyes. "Sing it again, Lerle," he softly implores, "It sounds so beautiful!" I sing. "Now, repeat it! Have you memorized it?" I nod.

Now Loos begins to sing the next motif of the Gurrelieder. He explains all the voices to me, the entire structure, the content, we work on it all day long until evening falls …

JAN SLIVINSKI

One day Jan Slivinski-Effenberger arrives from Paris. With his warmth, his happy disposition, his intelligent mind, he fills the whole apartment, makes life beautiful again. He has brought along a large suitcase and does not ever want to leave. He awakens the old dusty piano out of its silence and coaxes the most wonderful melodies out of it.

Loos looks at him, smiling. He does not hear him, but he watches him, how he sits comfortably at the piano and searchingly reaches for the chords. He makes a fascinating impression, his handsome, intelligent head slightly tilted back. This is the beginning of a happy period. The evil of people and everything depressing is forgotten. Every day is a new celebration. Jan Slivinski has such a strong personality.

Loos says: "Slivinski is a person who cannot stay long in one occupation. He always needs something new. But he is no dilettante, he has always fully completed each occupation he was in. He always was a master! Years ago, he was in charge of the Kaiser's library. Later, he became a piano virtuoso and singer. He worked together with Tagore to translate his poems from English into German. In Paris, he owned a large bookstore. Before that, he fought for the freedom of Poland. But his dream was to become a great singer. His voice was magnificent ... He almost lost it during the war ... That was his most painful ordeal ..."

Slivinski has become much more than a great singer ...

He is a whole person! Everyone who came to him, he has helped … He has discovered many artists … He went with Loos and Kokoschka into the small bars of Paris and tried to "save" poor young girls.

Also in Vienna, we went on pilgrimages together to the nightclubs. We usually ended our expeditions at the Reiss Bar. This is where the artists of Vienna congregate. All of them simply drop in there whenever they feel like it. Loos particularly enjoyed it when Hollitzer, who had such a unique personality, and was as powerful and impressive as a mighty tree, would sing …

LOOS AT WORK

The daily routine for Loos is as follows: In the morning at eight-thirty, Wipsi, the dog, is let into the room. He is a gentle alarm clock. Then Mitzi comes in with breakfast. This consists of a cup of coffee and two croissants with butter and honey. About this time, Suchanek – the carpenter – or the wall-paperer will often come to discuss some project with Loos. Other visitors are not allowed in, they have to wait in the dining room until Loos has bathed and dressed. The conversation with the workers, however, will often be carried on through the bathroom door.

Around eleven-thirty Loos takes a short walk. He strolls along the Kärntnerstrasse.

The highlight of the day is lunch at twelve-thirty. There are guests every day. Here, one can meet people from all over the world. Artists, scholars and those who would like to become them, clients, schoolboys, students, female dancers, grand ladies, demi-monde women. Loos knows how to bridge the gap between the most extreme opposites of an often motley assembly. He will often bring a guest with him even at the last moment.

After some black coffee, Loos rests for at least half an hour unconcerned whether or not guests are still there. Sometimes the guests simply stay seated at the table and continue chatting with one another. They do not bother him; he certainly cannot hear them.

Around three-thirty, a student or a co-worker will come to draw with him, or he drives out to a construction site.

His method of working would definitely not be taken seriously by many architects, and yet it is more productive than an office with a large staff.

One of my girlfriends, who had been working until recently in an architect's office in Munich and who is now working for Loos says: "Loos easily designs in half an hour what we often needed to spend weeks and months on in the office."

A young student of Loos, who had come right out of technical school, said after two months: "I have now learned more with Loos than I did during four years at technical school!"

The final drawings for the interior remodelling are made right at the carpenter's, in the room next to the workshop, and oftentimes the advice of the carpenter himself will be sought.

The best building designs by Loos, however, originate on the marble tops of coffee house tables.

MENUS...

The menus at Loos' are as international as the man himself. As part of the daily fare one finds:

"Pot-au-feu." Meat is cooked over a flame with lots of vegetables and spices. For example, mutton with cabbage or a stewing hen with a lot of vegetables, mushrooms and spices. If there are any leftovers, then a new vegetable is added to the pot, if there are still leftovers from the vegetable, then new meat is added and cooked.

Loos says: "'Pot-au-feu' is better on the second day than on the first, on the third better than on the second." A French tale claims that Henry IV supposedly kept this dish going for more than 120 years!

This dish is a real lifesaver for dear Mitzi. Loos often brings many unexpected guests at the last minute, so the "pot-au-feu" is usually all gone by the third day.

*

Another item of daily fare is porridge, prepared the English way:

Two coffee cups of oatmeal are sprinkled into three coffee cups of boiling water, cooked a few minutes, but not too long. "The flakes should indeed be soft, yet still lie individually on top of each other," says Loos. Cream and sugar are served separately with this dish.

Loos takes only a small portion on his plate, pours lots of cream over it and sprinkles sugar on top. "One has to be able to crunch on the sugar," he says.

Loos has long discussions with General K. in Prague who is of the same opinion as Loos that this healthy dish should be introduced into the Army; of course, milk would have to be used instead of cream.

The attempt fails; the soldiers do not like porridge.

*

Spinach or Savoy cabbage is washed well, cooked in water, put without any lard into a open saucepan for a minute to let the water evaporate, only then a bit of butter or lard is added.

Loos says: "Creamed spinach is only made so that one won't notice that it wasn't washed well!"

*

Before the soup, raw carrots that have been washed, cut lengthwise and placed in a water-glass on the table, are often eaten.

*

Schnitzel should never be pounded. Loos says: "The juice, the best part, gets beaten out!"

GROUNDS FOR DIVORCE

Loos enters the bathroom. His face grows red with anger. "You want to be my wife?" he shouts, "you, who have no respect for material? Who senselessly wastes it, lets it melt into nothing? You squanderer, you! Don't you know that I have spent my entire life fighting against the senseless, against ornamentation, against the waste of energy, against the waste of material? And you, my wife, dare to let this wonderful soap senselessly dissolve in the water?"

ONE SHOULD NOT PUT ONE'S MONEY IN THE BANK

I had never spoken to Loos about money matters. Still, I did dare once to timidly ask: "Dolfi, where do you have an account?" Loos looked at me in amazement. "Account? In a bank, so that I have to pay taxes? No, I prefer to spend my money myself ... Whenever I get some, I put it in my coat pocket and spend it. That is what it's for!"

"But Dolf," I say cautiously, "there isn't any more money in your coat pocket."

"Well, well," Loos says and takes out his wallet. "Yes, yes, you are right ... I did not even notice. Then write immediately to our housekeeper, Mitzi, she should go and get some money. And my student, Kulka ... Lerle," he cried out beaming. "I still have one hundred crowns there, and you tell me we have no money! We will go out for a nice lunch today!"

I do not find this at all reassuring. "But if Mitzi does not send us any money and Kulka doesn't either, what will we do then?"

Dolf shrugs his shoulders, irritated. "Just as God will not let the sparrows on the roof starve to death, he will not let me starve to death either ... My student Zladko Neumann, with whom I lived in Paris, asked me the same question once. All of our resources were used up, we each had three francs ... Zladko was desperate, but I told him the same I told you. Then we each bought a bottle of wine for two francs fifty and lay down in bed. That way we saved on heating, since it was winter. The next day a letter came from Kuhner, my client, with the following content:

'Dear Loos! All of my friends who had their homes remodelled at the same time I did have since had them remodeled three or four times while I am so satisfied with my apartment, which you did 25 years ago, that I hope to spend another fifty in it. Not only have you saved me a great deal of money but my apartment is more beautiful and more modern than those of my friends. I therefore beg you to accept the amount of 25,000 crowns, which I honestly feel I owe you. Yours thankfully ...'

You can imagine how we felt when that letter arrived. Zladko was quite beside himself ... We immediately arranged for big party of course ... The entire Montparnasse was invited – all the poor artists who had been starving just as we had. Also the young girls who were freezing on the street corners, a few countesses and counts and very rich people who were quite shocked at the company, but stayed anyway. In reality they were just happy to have a good time. Yes, and the 25,000 crowns? Yes, Lerle, quite a large part of it had of course disappeared by that time ... But I got more work soon after that. I just want to prove to you that my dear God does not abandon me. I am not afraid ...

And you, because you are my wife, do not need to be afraid either!"

Two days later, Kulka sent the amount of two thousand

crowns.

The thought of having a divinely-favored husband, who would never be forsaken by his Savior, was certainly uplifting, but it still did not satisfy my innate sense of practicality. What if this God ever did fail …! I decided to open an account at the next opportunity.

The next time we were in the city, we visited a client who, like all his clients, received Loos as his dear friend. Loos took him into the next room and whispered to him a while. He then came back in a good mood. I found in the afternoon his wallet again full.

"Just think," said Loos, "the good man immediately gave me some money when I asked for it."

"And you took it?"

"Of course!"

So it had come to the point that Loos would simply go and ask his clients for money – charity!

Loos, who noticed I was upset, looked at me in amazement: "You think this is charity? No! All … All my clients owe me money! … Think of the story I told you recently, the story that took place in Paris … But not just my clients, the whole world owes me money, because I have freed it from ornamentation, from unnecessary work! What the city of Vienna alone has saved by no longer having to nail ornaments onto the local council buildings, cannot even be expressed in money … They all owe me money," he continued murmuring before he lapsed into his midday nap …

I, however, was not satisfied with this answer. I tried to gain a better understanding of his business practices. Loos adapted his work according to the means of his clients. He was capable too, of creating something absolutely beautiful for little money. Loos was not only a great interior designer, he had an exceptional knowledge of materials as well. For example he would not hesitate to go out himself to select wood paneling for his clients instead of leaving it to his carpenters. He carefully chose pieces with the most beautiful wood grain. That way, even less expensive kinds of wood would not look lesser. (As a rule, however, he disliked Caucasian nut and rosewood and never used them).

Loos also preferred to work with ordinary craftsmen, who were inexpensive and with whom he could get along better than with cabinet-makers or engineers. Loos felt a strong human bond with these simple, good people, and they in turn considered Loos, despite their admiration for his great art, as one of them.

Loos knew of many small shops where one could buy valuable carpets, beautiful vases, lamps and other items for little money. It was always a great pleasure for him to take a client there and explain the value or worthlessness of individual items with everything right there.

Finally, Loos always thanked his client over and over for having given him the opportunity to realize one of his artistic ideas. He received as honorarium the usual 10 percent. But Loos usually went to his client whenever he needed money and so when work on a project was completed, he was not owed any more.

I succeeded in putting money into a bank instead of into his coat pocket. I just wanted to have a little security. I started to carry money over to the bank. Loos did not object. Money in a bank – that was something new! Sometimes, early in the morning, he would dress quickly and leave, whistling.

"Where are you going, Dolf?"

Loos, beaming: "To the bank, to get some money!"

Things continued like that for a while, the money in the bank started to dwindle, and one day there was nothing left.

"Why isn't there any more money in the bank?" Loos said, quite surprised, "you did put it in there!"

He thought one could now go and get money for an unlimited time.

"Or did the tax authorities confiscate the money?" he asked suspiciously. "See, I told you right off. One should not put one's money in the bank ..."

MARBLE

Every marble that Loos uses has a story. This one I experienced first-hand:

Loos visits a marble quarry in Switzerland. Here he finds blocks of Cipolino marble. It is brittle stone because streaks of foreign metal ores run through it. Loos, however, knows that this diseased marble in particular is incredibly beautiful. He wants to buy it, it costs almost nothing. Since Loos has no money at all, he convinces a client to buy it. The buyer is quite astonished when four blocks instead of three arrive from Switzerland. The following note is enclosed: "Dear Herr B.! We took the liberty of sending a fourth block along for free since it was just lying in our way ..." There is so much marble that Loos, who had planned on paneling his client's dining room with it, changes his mind. "It would be a shame," he says, "only to use part of it."

A year passes. Loos builds the Müller house in Prague. Dr. Müller buys the marble for the large hall. Tumultuous days follow – the marble specialists in Prague refuse to cut the stone. They are afraid it will break – Loos will not give up. Finally, an Italian says he is willing to take over the job, although without any guarantee. Loos says the stone will have to be put onto concrete slabs and pieced together if it breaks.

Despite his optimism Loos is very nervous. One day passes, a second – will it work, will it not work? It works!

The Italian informs us. The slabs have been cut, only a few show cracks, splits. Most of them are whole. Loos rejoices. We immediately take the car to the workshop. The slabs are lying there on long tables, but they are gray and colourless! I am disappointed. Loos, however, laughs. They have not been polished yet. Look! He takes some water and pours it over the gray stone. A miracle occurs! The wet marble gleams a deep green; blue, violet and reddish-yellow veins of colour run through it in soft waves. It looks like the sea.

A VISIT TO FRAU X.

Shortly after we are married we visit Frau X. She is a good friend of Loos and one of his benefactors. I have read and heard a lot about her and have always wanted very much to meet her. I make myself look particularly nice. A black velvet dress … and I finish by donning a little hat with a veil.

A number of prominent people are here as guests. Frau X. is like a queen at her court, she leads the discussion, bringing individuals into the conversation as she sees fit. Is it just an accident or is it on purpose? She ignores me, as if I were not there. The conversation is light and witty, it jumps from person to person. I try to join in … I fail, Frau X. immediately cuts me off … So I sit, lonely and abandoned, fighting back my tears …

My husband is deeply involved in a discussion with an artist. Since he is hard of hearing, any conversation is difficult, I do not want to disturb him. Time passes … Finally we leave. At home I throw myself on the bed crying my heart out.

"Oh Lerle, oh Lerle," he says, "what happened?"

"You know," I sob, "I realize that next to you I am nothing, but at Frau X.'s I was less than nothing!"

My husband sits beside me and gently strokes my hair. "Don't let it bother you, Lerle! When I was there with Elsie, when I was there with Bessie, when I was there with Lina, my wives always came back home crying … Don't let it get to you, Lerle, she is only jealous I didn't also marry her!"

NEWSPAPERS

Loos sits for hours on end buried in his newspapers and is not available to talk to anyone. He reads English, French and German newspapers, although he does not understand much French. He reads the newspaper with the same attention from beginning to end, only leaving out the novel section. He says: "Studying the classified ads is just as important as reading the political news. From them you learn the needs and the surpluses of a country."

WHY DO YOU ONLY WANT A BED?

"Dolfi, why don't you want a couch in the bedroom, why only a bed?"

"The bed, Lerle, the bedroom is the most sacred, most private matter, no stranger should be allowed to profane this sanctuary … The bedroom should not have a door opening onto a living room!"

"But Dolfi, if there is very little room in an apartment?"

"Then the bedroom should be very small … Just enough room for a double bed … The closets are built in or placed in the hallway."

"But if there isn't any room for them either?"

Dolf looks up annoyed from his newspaper. His glasses have slid down his nose. "Let me read, Lerle, take the dog for a walk!"

THE DIFFERENCE

I have a terrible mess in my room. When I return from a walk, I find Loos standing in the middle of the still un-tidied room. He looks at me and asks:

"Do you know the essential difference between a proletarian and an aristocrat?

I silently shake my head.

"A proletarian leaves everything lying around. He says: the personnel is there to tidy up. An aristocrat puts everything away himself, it is embarrassing for him to have a stranger, an employee, handle his private things …"

THE MÜLLER HOUSE

The Müller house is growing. Loos orders an overhang of a half a centimeter on the house. He drives away. When he returns, the overhang measures an entire centimeter instead of only a half. Loos is beside himself and has the extra half a centimeter taken off all the way around the house. To the left of the main entrance is a door. In this room, the master of the house can receive visitors whom he does not wish to take into the house. Here there is a desk, a bench, the room is covered in dark lilac wallpaper; a large space is left un-papered, and this is where Loos had a gigantic map put up. A lovely, colourful interruption – and at the same time a guest who is waiting can pass the time pleasantly.

A double glass door leads into the front hall, which is panelled in white wood. The ceiling is low; Loos, however, still finds it too high and so has it painted dark blue at the last minute. A nice contrast to the white wood. Now come three, four steps. Then, an overwhelming sight – the large main room. Loos has intentionally made the entrance intimate and low so that the impact of the main room is intensified. He says it is wrong, when one opens the door, to immediately, without a transition, be standing in the largest room of the house. To the left, situated between two blocks of green marble, is a sofa covered in lilac upholstery. On top of each of the marble blocks, which house the heating, Loos had wanted to put an old Japanese wooden figurine, but he found none that he would have liked.

The client has a whole life ahead of him, he has time "to grow into" the house and has room to acquire many beautiful objects that will fit into the house. That is what Loos thinks and so he gives up the search for the wooden figurines.

A narrow staircase in the main room leads up to the boudoir. A window looks down from this room into the main room so that the lady of the house can observe those arriving without herself being noticed. A small, delicate woman, she will make a grand and imposing impression as she walks down the stairs toward her guests.

On the right side of the main room, a couple of steps lead up to a dining room. The extra space that this has created under the dining room allows for light from the street to reach the utility rooms in the cellar. The ceiling of the dining room is made of dark mahogany. A subsequent client also wanted to have such a ceiling in his dining room. Loos said: "I was able to put a wood ceiling in this small room because it opens out onto the main room. In a small, enclosed room, this ceiling would look like the lid of a coffin. I'll make your ceiling run through the dining room and the men's sitting room, then it is possible." (Loos did, as a matter of fact, connect the men's sitting room and the dining room in this new apartment and put up a continuous mahogany ceiling, which looked wonderful).

Dr. Müller's dining room is, like all Loos' dining rooms, not very large. Loos says: "It is large enough as long as the maid can comfortably serve a meal. There is no need for more room than that." The round granite table required a lot of planning. It was constructed in such a way that with a few guests one round mahogany tabletop could be put out, and two tabletops when there were more guests. The chairs are copies of Chippendale chairs.

Next to the dining room is a small room, the pantry, and then comes the kitchen; it is surprisingly small. Cooking is done here following the American system. Everything is within easy reach and has its own designated place. Loos uses the kitchen of a dining car as a model. A light is installed above the stove. The window is high. Loos explains, smiling: "It is unnecessary for the cook to be able to look out of the window while cooking."

When the house was completed, the following article appeared in the Prager Tagblatt on February 15, 1931:

"During the past three months, the Müller house, located across from the Norbert Church in Štreschowitz, has become a popular place to visit. It was built by Adolf Loos. The guest book boasts such names as Marcel Ray, Karl Kraus, Emil Ludwig, Machar, Filene, Ilja Ehrenburg, and Arnold Schönberg. Karin Michaelis wrote the following to Loos after having toured the house: "Dear friend, the house in Prague is by far, far, far the most beautiful one that you have built. If there were such a thing as a precious stone that was more elegant and more valuable than diamonds, emeralds or sapphires, I would compare this house with it. If I were Kokoschka, I would want to paint twelve pictures in it, if I were Pavlova, I would only want to dance there."

AT THE NUDIST BATHHOUSE

Frau Erna calls me on the telephone and asks: "Wouldn't you like to go bathing with us today? We are going to the Strohgasse ... Do bring your husband along too!"

"Strohgasse?" says Loos, immediately knitting his brows. "You want to go bathing with a bunch of lunatics? That's that nudist club bathhouse ..."

"If Erna is going," I reply, my curiosity peaking, "it is definitely healthy, moral and nice."

"Healthy, moral perhaps ... but nice?! Brrr ..." Loos shudders with disgust. "I have never seen such a group of tense, unnatural people as I have there ... And yet they only carry on extremely moral conversations. The slightest flirting is forbidden ... The whole thing is hypocritical and unnatural, nowhere have I ever found such a strained conversational tone. The people there all think they are so superior because they talk about art, literature and the theater while in the nude. Those are not natural, free human beings at all, just undressed Philistines!"

"Just don't talk to them then," I plead, "I would like so much to see these strange people."

"Alright," says Loos, suddenly staring at me with a serious, wide-eyed look, "we will go. But I am warning you: there will be no backing out, that will be your punishment!"

We go. I am already feeling a tremendous urge to run when a red-haired, skinny, hunchbacked man, who is wearing less than nothing, hospitably shows us to the changing rooms.

"You will hardly find any beauties here," Loos whispers to me, "ugly people have the peculiar trait of wanting to be seen in the nude."

I am searching desperately for an excuse to leave. Loos, who has suspected this, forces me to stay by giving me a stern look.

Thank God, there is something resembling a towel in the dressing room. I wrap myself up tightly in it, determined not to give up this utensil without a fight. I leave the room feeling a little more self-confident.

Loos walks towards me dressed in paradisiacal garb so totally at ease and comfortable as if he were wearing a fine well-tailored suit. He casts me a scathing, disparaging look but does not say anything.

We enter the bathing hall. Groups of nothing less than beautiful people, some sitting on benches, some standing, women and men, seem to be carrying on profound conversations. Their facial expressions are serious and dignified but their poses seem curiously chosen and their voices agitated. They look like bad extras to me. Noticing us come in, their eyes fall on us, and reluctantly settle on me. I am dying of embarrassment and wrap myself up even tighter in my towel.

"You are causing an unpleasant scene with your towel," Loos says scornfully, "just drop it and no one will stare at you anymore. Here among the nudists you have the same effect as a naked person among the clothed!"

Sure enough, as soon as I drop my towel all eyes turn away

indifferently and pay me no more attention. Loos pulls me into the water. His face brightens when he sees a young blond man. It is our journeyman carpenter Josef.

"How lucky to meet you here," exclaims Loos; not in the least embarrassed, he genially extends his hand. "I had wanted to go the workshop today anyway. Are the veneers finished yet?"

The carpenter nods. "May I introduce you? Josef – my wife!"

Since I am not particularly thrilled by this introduction, I head back to dry land while Loos continues his discussion of the veneers. Distraught, I pace back and forth. Thank God, Erna comes towards me. She ceremoniously introduces me to a few people and offers me a cigarette. The red-headed hunchbacked man shows up again. He looks at me with a scathing gaze.

"You really ought to enroll in one of our exercise classes," he says in a high falsetto voice, "I can see several fat deposits on you."

I force myself to a polite smile even though I feel rather like crying. Luckily, Erna has initiated a conversation about art and literature. I try to also express my opinion, everyone listens politely, yet I have the feeling that no one really cares at all about me.

Loos climbs out of the water. He remains standing a long while on the top step, slowly and carefully removing the water off his body so as not to carry any more water into the dressing room than is absolutely necessary. He then motions to me to do the same.

"I am really very glad," he says cheerily, "we came here, otherwise I would not have gotten to meet the carpenter. And you," he continues, "did you have a good time?"

I remain silent. Loos makes an innocent face and whistles to himself.

THE COMPANIONWAY

Loos meets client X. on the street. "Just imagine," he exclaims, "a visitor to my villa yesterday complained about the narrow staircase, and do you know what he compared it with? A ship's companionway!"

"With a companionway?" Loos cries out excitedly. "Did he really say that? When you see that man again, shake his hand for me and tell him someone has finally really understood my architecture. The ship is the model for a modern house. There space is totally utilized, no unnecessary waste of space! Nowadays, with building sites being so expensive, every inch of space must be used ... I have not only got rid of ornamentation, I have discovered a new way of building. Building into space, the *Raumplan*, spatial design. I do not build in flat planes, I build in space, in three-dimensions. This is the way I manage to accommodate more rooms into a house. The bathroom does not need to have a ceiling as high as the living room ... The rooms are nested into each other, each has a height and size corresponding to its purpose. The staircase, however, connects the separate, different levels ... A person has to be able to walk comfortably ... a staircase is not made so that couples go rushing past each other. It does not need to be any wider than a ship's companionway ...

"Unfortunately the architects of today don't know yet how to think in terms of space. In a hundred years it will be different! Seven hundred years ago there was a man who could think in terms of space – it was Dante in his 'Divine Comedy' ..."

LOOS IS ILL

Loos is ill. We have not heard anything from Karl Kraus for weeks. Suddenly he calls from Berlin. He asks how Loos is feeling. He does not call just once, he calls daily.

A few weeks later, Kraus is in Vienna. He drops by daily at seven in the evening to see Loos. "At breakfast time," jokes Loos, since Kraus sleeps during the day and works at night.

During this period all other visitors must be kept away. Loos is happy to see Kraus so often. He says: "I did not know at all that Kraus has such a Jewish sense of family."

"But Dolf, you are not even at all related to him."

Loos nods, annoyed: "Oh, but I am, I am … a relative by choice …"

IT IS NOT THAT EASY

We are walking down the Kärntnerstrasse. I contemplatively watch the girls strolling by. This irritates Loos.

"Yes, yes, you middleclass women think the life these girls lead is so easy! One of you should try standing out here and asking for 100 schillings ... you would soon find out something ... You can always find someone to go with you for free ... but for money –?!"

A TOTAL MESS AND AN HONORARY GRAVE

Loos is still sick. The doctors find his condition very serious. We take him to a well-known Viennese sanatorium. The ward rounds are at 5 o'clock.

"How are you feeling here with us?" asks the head physician.

"A total mess," says Loos, his voice dying away.

The head physician looks at the junior physician, the junior physician at the assistant and the assistant at the nurse. She helplessly shrugs her shoulders.

"Yes, yes, a total mess – this place is like the Balkans!" exclaims Loos loudly. "I'm just surprised they don't put roux in the compote."

"What on earth has happened?" asks the astounded head physician.

Loos replies, "They serve hot milk with your tea here!"

The doctor orders Loos a sedative.

From now on, however, cold milk is served with tea throughout the entire sanatorium …

Loos' condition worsens. One day he asks me to give him a sheet of paper and a pencil. With a great deal of effort and a trembling hand he draws a block on it and writes beneath it: 'Born Brünn, died Vienna.' Look, Lerle, this is my tombstone!"

"How can one be having such depressing thoughts?!" To

cheer him up, I draw four little blocks around the first and write the names of his wives on them.

Loos looks at the drawing and says with a fading voice, "Not even when I am dead can I expect to be left in peace?!"

He takes a fresh sheet of paper and sketches a new block on it. Then he presses the drawing into my hand and dictates to me short and to the point: "Tombstone of gray granite; size, ..." – Loos thinks for a moment –, "size not specified, it depends on how much money is available ... It should not be too small though or it will look like an over-sized inkwell, and," he adds in conclusion, "write honorary grave on it!"

I look at Loos for a moment, astonished. Loos, who has guessed my thoughts, smiles. I can see in his eyes that the old rogue is being sarcastic and cynical. "Just write down honorary grave. The Viennese are going to have such a bad conscience when it comes to me that I am sure I will get an honorary grave!"

With that he turns himself over towards the wall, five minutes later he has fallen asleep. The very next day he regains his health.

THE ENCYCLOPEDIA

"What are you looking up in the encyclopedia, Dolfi?"

"I'm not looking up anything."

"What are you doing then?"

"I'm reading."

"In the encyclopedia?"

"Yes, it's the most interesting reading material I know of. Far more interesting than any old novel!"

LOOS SAYS...

"Little has changed in my architecture over 30 years. But I am a lot shorter, just as the earlier car differentiates itself from that of today mainly in that it is a lot lower."

"I am a Communist. The difference between me and a Bolshevik is only that I want to turn all the people into aristocrats, whereas he wants to turn them all into proletarians ..."

When one of his female clients asks during a discussion about her dining room decor if Loos wouldn't consider making the buffet a little larger, Loos answers: "That is what you want? I find that the larger the buffet, the more stupid the woman is!"

Loos is sitting having dinner with one of his female admirers. Suddenly she says: "Oh, forgive me, Herr Loos, I drank out of your glass by mistake."

Loos replies perfectly straight-faced: "That is quite alright, dear Frau X., I am not terrified of anything!"

AT PENSION Z. IN VIENNA...

We are sitting at the big communal table of the hotel. And facing us is a lady with her grown-up daughter. They bow their heads way down over their plates. They slurp their soup. I can tell that Loos finds this visibly disturbing. The meat is served … The two ladies hold their knife close to the blade. They spread out their elbows.

Loos mumbles: "So that they won't cut their fingers."

The meat has been eaten, but some gravy remains. Then something terrible happens: Using their knives, the ladies slurp up the gravy.

Loos cannot contain himself any longer. "I fear, dear madam, that you are going to cut your mouth," and with a face permeated with the seriousness of a holy mission, he begins: "Years ago I published an article called 'The Introduction of Occidental Culture into Austria,' you should read it … By the way, where do you come from anyway?"

"I'm Turkish."

Loos breathes a sigh of relief: "Lucky for you!"

THE MANDL HOUSE

Herr Mandl tells me how his house came to be. "I was thinking," says Herr Mandl, "about buying some real estate in the Blaasgasse but I couldn't make up my mind. An acquaintance gave me the advice I should look up Adolf Loos. Loos drove out to Döbling with me, looked at the house and simply said: 'Buy it, by all means, buy it.' I still could not decide, however, as the house was old, a real shambles. I visited Loos again. I asked: 'Just why should I buy this house?' Loos replied: 'The location is good, I have some new ideas precisely for this project.' Loos takes a paper napkin and sketches on it. 'First of all, the guts of the house have to be removed. Everything inside will have to go. The right exterior wall of the house will have to be removed.' We immediately started work on the house. It's standing there, with only three walls. It was late in the fall, construction was halted. Loos left for Nice. It rained, it snowed, it stormed. In the spring, Loos returns, construction is resumed. 'I get my best ideas when I'm building – I never make plans.' He creates a palatial hall that rises up two stories high –, the house is unrecognizable.

"One day Loos is sitting across from me at the desk and stares at me for a long while. Finally, he says: 'I know now how the interior will have to look. For you there is only one material: oak.' I jump up, saying: 'Herr Architect, may I say du to you? Do you know I have always loved oak?' Loos hugs me and says: 'I have known that already for the longest time;

you do not need to tell me.' But then I became again a little anxious. Won't it cost a fortune? Loos: 'You will get that amount back many times over if you ever sell the house, and then I will build you a new, even far more beautiful one.' Loos would be proven right. I sold the house for many times over what I paid for it.

But there were a few differences between us. I had some antique furniture and a few works by Kolo Moser. I furnished the upstairs rooms with them. Loos did not like these pieces at all. If visitors were at the house, and Loos were present, he would never fail to mention in a most disapproving tone: 'These people already had this furniture.' Originally, he wanted to have the columns in the dining room constructed out of rough brick. I would not agree to it and so marble columns were put in. Loos sighed when he saw them and said: 'I never should have given in; rough brick would have created an entirely different effect.' But the hall made of polished light oak looked stunning. I am convinced that my house is the most beautiful of all, in the end it had become what both of us had imagined. Loos was not my architect, I was not his client – we built it together."

THE CARINTHIAN BALL IN VIENNA

"Lerle, let's go, Mitzi, our housekeeper Mitzi, is on the organizing committee and is getting us a large private box. You know, Lerle, that Mitzi would be very offended if we didn't go; we only need to stay half an hour, we owe that much to our Mitzi."

I am wearing a red and white checked Dirndl, Dolfi a brown leather jacket. Mitzi greets us in a Carinthian folk costume, it looks wonderful on her.

"I never realized that she is so beautiful," Dolf whispers to me.

The folk costume procession is colourful and lively. We are sitting in the private box with Mitzi's husband, who is a specialist in refrigerators, his nephew, an apprentice carpenter, a retailer of fancy foods, a charming young girl and a waitress. Dolfi is in the best of moods.

The folk costume procession breaks up into dance couples. I start to get up and want to leave, as agreed. Dolfi's eyes are still enthusiastically fixed on individual country beauties.

"I have been to a lot of balls, but I have never seen so much natural beauty anywhere!" he exclaims. "None of them are wearing any make-up, many of them look so elegant that the city girls can just run and hide." He would not dream of leaving now. A good-looking tall country lad asks me for a dance. I glance over to my husband, he nods. "Go ahead and dance, Lerle, have a good time!"

The young man is a shoemaker and asks me where I am working. I say that I am a waitress here in Vienna. The young man asks me for a second dance. I quickly glance over at our table, Loos has disappeared. I am not worried and continue dancing. The shoemaker comes over again and again, asking me to dance, my face is getting red from lying. Then Mitzi approaches.

"Madame," she calls out from a distance, "and oh God, Franzl!", before I can say anything, Franzl now realizes who I am and, upset, quickly disappears.

"Where is my husband?" I ask. Mitzi does not know. We go through the ballrooms searching for him. Finally, in the last one, we find him sitting, a pretty girl from Mondsee on each side. Sitting in the corner are two lads glaring in anger at Loos. He sees us and waves.

"You know, Lerle, we absolutely have to go to Mondsee sometime soon," he says beaming. "In the spring they have a big festival, a real Walpurgisnacht. People jump through the bonfires, they bake a special kind of cake … Lerle, we really have to go there!" Then to the two girls: "Tomorrow, ladies, you must both come over to my house for lunch, you don't mind, do you, Lerle?" I indicate I do not.

At this point, one of the country lads jumps up, furiously pounding his fist on the table. "But we mind, that girl you're flirting with is my fiancée, sir!"

Indignant, the girl jumps up. "This man was behaving very properly!"

"Sure, but he was talkin' to you the whole time!"

"That's because he's smarter than you are, you stupid lout!"

And then all hell breaks loose! Mitzi and I grab Dolf under each arm and quickly usher him outside.

"What happened, Lerle?" he asks, because he did not hear. "Why doesn't she want to come for lunch? ... Why?"

CHAIRS

"We do not have any good chairs," Loos often says. He tries once himself to design a chair – it fails. He suggests that Thonet sponsor a chair-designing contest. Thonet follows his advice, but does not choose Loos to be a juror. This upsets Loos.

Loos does not like furniture made of steel. He tolerates it for the waiting room of a doctor's office or in a shoe store but never uses it himself. It is too mechanical for his taste. Loos remarks sarcastically: "A new discovery has been made in Central Europe. Metal chairs! How ridiculous! Even the good old French king Dagobert had a throne constructed according to the same principles of this 'new invention'. But the era of monarchs is long since gone. One can see that even in art by the fact that a Ludwig II of Bavaria was no longer capable of forcing someone like Richard Wagner onto the stupid masses, whereas in the old days, the sovereign imposed on the population the artists of his liking."

Loos took me once to an old church in Nancy. He showed me the chair of an ecclesiastical prince – it was made out of metal! He is constantly occupied with the chair problem. What he would really like is to have Japanese basket weavers come to Europe and have them weave him some chairs. But it would cost too much. Loos uses English chairs in his dining rooms, Chippendales. Since his chair-maker died though, he cannot find anyone who can really copy Chippendales well.

We are in Hall. Loos is sitting in front of the hotel. Suddenly he becomes excited – jumps up –, closely examines the wicker chair, sits down again testing it – gets up again! An inscription on the back of the chair reads: Herlitz, Scharnstein. Loos waves down a cab. "Lerle, get in." We drive to Scharnstein. Herr Herlitz is a simple man. Loos looks over all of his furniture. "Good, good," he says. On a tabletop, he draws the new chair – without any arms. A model is made. Loos is not satisfied. It takes three or four additional models before he is finally pleased. He has the seat and back of the chair covered in coloured oilcloth upholstery. The edge of the upholstery is finished off with a row of round-headed tacks, making it look like a fine gold chain. Loos places these wicker chairs, each upholstered in a different colour, in a dining room with yellow travertine marble.

EVERYONE SHOULD BE HIS OWN BOSS

Loos says: "I'm against any kind of political party; against partisanship. The city housing projects are only built in order to promote party support. The people get herded together so they will vote for the party.

Everyone should have his own little house and his own garden. Rental property should be reserved solely for businesses. In England, they have already created business districts in the cities; the people live in cottages in the suburbs. Business hours are from 9 to 4 and after that everyone is his own boss. Humankind will not be truly happy until it can live like that. Rich and poor; the lower middle-class worker has his own little house just like the rich businessman … and everyone is his own boss. That is how things should be!"

EMIL LUDWIG IN PRAGUE

"Lerle, Emil Ludwig is in Prague, go see him, send him my best regards and ask him if he would like to take a tour of my house here in Prague."

"Dolfi, I can't do that; I don't even know Emil Ludwig!"

Loos is not feeling very well. He sits up in bed, his eyes are fixed on me.

"What can't you do, Lerle?"

I stutter: "Simply go visit the famous Emil Ludwig ..."

"Lerle, shame on you, you never want to do anything for me anymore. You're lazy, so lazy!" He sighs.

"Well, I will gladly go, but will he even agree to see me?"

Loos is truly angry. "If you tell him you are my wife, definitely! – By the way, he's an old friend of mine. Dolfi chuckles softly to himself. "I remember, it's been several years now, he turned up once in our circle. Emil Ludwig! Karl Kraus said about him: 'He's dark and soft like a Blüthner grand piano.' We did not take him very seriously. Yes, Lerle, back then he wasn't any older than you ... He later visited me one more time with his wife. Rumor had it in Vienna that she was an English aristocrat. Do you remember that little book with the Scottish tartan plaids in it? Every aristocrat has one of those patterns in his family crest. I wanted to really please her so I handed her the book and said, 'Surely your crest is in there too.' She looked at it astonished because she was no aristocrat! The Viennese had been grossly exaggerating as usual. But do go now, Lerle. I'm tired and want to sleep."

My nervousness has strangely disappeared. "Just tell me please why I should actually show Emil Ludwig the house?" Loos is very surprised by my question. "But Lerle, didn't you say yourself that Emil Ludwig is a famous man? All prominent people of our time should see my house."

I go to the Hotel Steiner and leave my calling card. A short while later, a tall, black-haired man with a very pleasant, soft voice does indeed appear.

"Madame, how very nice to see you again. Excuse me," he says, as I come closer, "You're not at all the Frau Loos I know." It turned out he had thought I was Lina, Loos' first wife. "And how is Loos doing?" he asks cordially, after the mistake has been cleared up, "I have not seen him in twenty-five years."

A little embarrassed, I excuse his absence with his illness. We take a cab and drive to the Müller villa that Loos built in Prague. On the way, I have a wonderful idea: Emil Ludwig writes the memoirs of famous men, so couldn't he write a Loos biography? … Stuttering and clumsy, I make my proposal. Emil Ludwig knits his brow, then gently shakes his head, and replies in his soft voice:

"Loos … Loos is not famous enough … he's no Napoleon."

"No, that he is not," I think bitterly to myself, "he has not killed anyone, all he has ever wanted is to free people from the burden of unnecessary labor …" The rest of the drive to the villa is marked by an uncomfortable atmosphere. Luckily we arrive at the house before too long. In silence, we tour the rooms. Out on the terrace, from which one can see all of Prague, we remain standing for a long, long time.

Then Emil Ludwig says slowly, "It is too bad they just finished my house in Switzerland … Really too bad! I should have had Loos build it …"

"Well, Lerle, how was it, how did Emil Ludwig like my house?"

I tell him all about the visit.

"Yes, Lerle," says Loos, as I have finished telling him, "someday a lot of people will regret that they did not have me build them a house, but by that time it will definitely be too late!" He sighs … Suddenly he turns to me, "I hope that in your enthusiasm you did not talk him into writing a biography about me! I would gladly build him a house, but if he ever wrote a biography about me, I could never forgive him!"

LOOS AND THOMAS BAŤA

Loos wants to found a school for architecture. Five prominent men are to sign a petition: Heinrich Mann, Valéry Larbaud, Arnold Schönberg, Karl Kraus and, as the fifth, Loos would like to have Baťa. Loos considers him one of the most influential men of our time ... But Baťa refuses. Loos wires him, calls him on the telephone, to no avail ... Baťa refuses. Loos feels very insulted. He says: "I'll never forgive him for this!"

We are sitting in the Mánes Restaurant in Prague. Baťa is at the next table. Loos jumps up. Even though he does not know him personally, nevertheless he rushes right over to him. "Why didn't you sign the petition for the school?"

Baťa makes an unassuming gesture as if to say, it would be a great honor for me, but I am, after all, just a simple man!

Loos: "I've seen your factory – one of the greatest plants there is anywhere! You are a real philanthropist! Everyone should take a trip to Zlín and see your factory. You are a master of organization ... You could be a government leader!" He shakes Baťa's hand in recognition. But Baťa remains unmoved. He doesn't sign.

When we are alone again, I ask Loos: "Why don't you actually wear any shoes from Baťa?"

Loos makes a guilty face. "You know I never wear ready-made clothes!"

COLOURS

Loos says: "I do not understand architects! They are always afraid of using strong colours beside each other.

I find that a meadow full of flowers is very beautiful, and yet every flower is a different colour.

Colours can be used together in a room in exactly the same way as long as they are as pure as the colours of a meadow of flowers. It is only the blended colours, the dirtied colours, that are not pretty …"

I AM A COSMOPOLITAN

A big exhibition is being held abroad. Loos is also represented. His plans are exhibited alongside the work of the Austrian artists. Loos does not know anything about the whole affair. His student, Kulka, in Vienna had sent in the plans. We happen to be in Prague and Loos is attacked by the Czechoslovak artists.

"You are a Czechoslovak, Loos, how is it that are you are exhibiting with the Austrians, it has caused a lot of ill will here. You are losing your popularity with the people here by doing this!"

Loos, who has no idea of what they are talking about, has the situation explained to him first, then he replies, shaking his head: "The Czechoslovaks think I am a Czechoslovak because I was born in Brno and came from there. The Austrians say I've lived in Vienna for so many years, the Germans say I am German because I speak their language, in France, they suggested that I become a naturalized citizen because I love their country so much, my English wife always said I dressed better than an Englishman … ," and smiling: "I am neither one nor the other. I am a cosmopolitan, as is every true European …"

THE SIXTIETH BIRTHDAY (10. DECEMBER 1930)

Loos' sixtieth birthday is celebrated in Prague. The citizens of Prague are particularly proud of the fact that Loos, the great Loos, is a Czechoslovak citizen and will not be denied the opportunity to honor him in a grand manner.

Dr. Markalous, the Czechoslovak journalist and writer, has made arrangements for a celebration in the Společenský klub. A large tea party takes place.

Loos is ceremoniously welcomed and handed a bouquet of red roses. Suddenly, on the threshold to the banquet hall, Loos stops.

"Quick, Lerle, go back to the Hotel Steiner and get Karl Kraus. He will not come on his own, he hates public celebrations ... I would really like for him to be here."

Just at that moment a fanfare sounds and the doors open, it is out of the question now for me to leave. We walk in. But right beside the door, amid the other guests, stands Karl Kraus.

We are led to two chairs, thrones of a sort.

One architect gives a speech and is followed by a second. Loos can tell by the way they move their mouths that the one is speaking German and the other Czech. He interrupts the second speaker, saying merrily: "Gentlemen, it doesn't really matter in which language you honor me in because I am deaf!" After a while, he interrupts the speaker again and begins to give his own speech. He points out that a lot can be learned about a culture from looking at their bathrooms and toilets.

The overly ceremonious atmosphere gives way to natural, good-natured merriment. Later, we are served tea. Sitting beside Loos is his friend, General Klecanda. A great number of prominent people have come to celebrate Loos.

The evening is spent at Dr. Müller's in the villa Loos built. Loos conducts the conversation. The guests assemble in the large main room, then proceed into the dining room. How wonderful the marble table looks with the round mahogany tabletop. At Loos' express wish, no tablecloth has been laid out, only little mats. He says:

"The most elegant tablecloth is a beautiful tabletop!"

After dinner some of the guests retire into the women's drawing room and some into the men's drawing room; both rooms are nice and cozy.

Karl Kraus, the unapproachable, is telling amusing anecdotes. Machar reports about Masaryk, to whose home he was invited for lunch.

The evening is charming and jovial … it is hard to leave such wonderful hosts.

On the occasion of his sixtieth birthday, Loos received, in addition to his yearly pension, an honorarium from the Czechoslovak Department of Education for his outstanding artistic achievements.

AT THE PARK HOTEL

We are in Vienna again! This time we have taken a room at the Park Hotel out in Hietzing. Life here is pleasant and nice. Kulka drops by in the mornings to discuss business matters. The Kuhner house is currently under construction. Guests come over for tea in the afternoons. Kiki, a sweet little Japanese dog, enjoys the surroundings too. Unfortunately, Kiki has not been house-trained yet.

"You are going to have to get her into the habit of going out on the balcony," says Loos gently.

Kiki gets locked out on the balcony for hours on end. This method works. Kiki is house-trained. But, miracle of miracles, there aren't any spots that are even slightly damp out on the balcony either! The mystery soon finds an explanation. One evening, just as the dance music is beginning to float up into our rooms, the waiter from downstairs bursts in:

"Madame," he says loudly, gasping for breath, "there is terrible agitation downstairs, it has – has been raining on our best tables! I tried to calm down the guests by saying that Madame was probably watering her flowers, but since they couldn't see any flowers, they didn't believe it and got very upset!"

During the course of this somewhat bewildering conversation we have both gone out to the terrace, here we find Kiki pressing her body up against the railing, barking happily at me because she undoubtedly thinks I approve of her good idea!

The waiters continue being friendly to us, despite this rather embarrassing incident, because they all love Kiki! And she is quite a clever little character. The instant she senses someone watching her, she immediately starts to flirt and do the craziest tricks; if no one pays any attention to her, she pouts and gets angry. Loos loves her. There are often jealousy scenes between this cunning little lady dog and me. I decide that our next dog will be a male, totally disregarding the fact that Kiki is still in the best of health and there is no reason to give her away.

Loos has discovered a young painter.

He commissions a picture from him, which, says Loos, will in fact have to be painted on a wall. It will be for Herr B.'s dining room. Herr B. has the misfortune to live exactly opposite a factory. It is a depressing view, particularly from the dining room. Loos puts up sheer golden yellow curtains at the windows which, when drawn, drench the room in sunlight. On the wall opposite the windows, he leaves a large part open in the light wood paneling. Here on the wall, which beforehand must be carefully prepared with egg whites, the young painter Aigner paints his picture. It shows three strong figures, peasants, navigating a small boat. A few pieces of driftwood stick up out of the water. The picture is simple but is interesting in its composition and spatial distribution. Loos likes its simplicity. Still, he is not entirely satisfied. "This picture has to be so impressive," says Loos, "that the poor man who lives here forgets that he has an ugly factory right in front of his nose and thinks that this picture is the view from his window. It must seem to be that close. That fresh and vibrant in its colours. This is only possible if it is painted directly on the wall, without a frame, without glass. We are approaching an era when frescoes will become modern again." There are still a few things in the design of the picture that he does not find quite right. He has them changed. "You must go to Paris, young man," he repeats again and again, "an artist suffocates here in Vienna!"

THE ELECTIONS

When the elections were being held in Austria four years ago and Loos was asked whom he would vote for – Loos is Czechoslovak – he answered: "Starhemberg."

"But your ideas are more in line with the Social Democrats!" Loos nods.

"And you would still vote for Starhemberg?"

Loos: "Yes, because I think Starhemberg is a capable human being."

"And if you could determine the ballot list by yourself?"

"Karl Kraus."

LAPIS LAZULI

We are at a small spa again taking the waters. We are staying at the best hotel – but in the worst room! Kiki, the dog, Loos and I. Kiki loves it and constantly wants to go for rides in a hackney-carriage. She always has to sit beside the coachman and be the center of attention. But if you dare not look at her, she will bark like crazy. Otherwise, she sits quietly, proud, unapproachable.

We have run low on money, I am in a bad mood, Loos is bored, he also does not like the taste of the water from the spring! One day Loos comes home very distressed.

"I met Doctor X., can you imagine, Lerle, he lent me 250 dollars 25 years ago and now he wants to have the money back. What do you think about that, Lerle?" Loos is outraged. I say nothing. I sigh and contemplate our predicament. Pay up or leave. Maybe the dear man will forget about it and we will not meet again for another 25 years.

Then Frau W. bursts into the room. She is a charming young woman, an ardent admirer of Loos. "Loos," she rejoices, "I have a wonderful piece of news for you! Dr. X. would like you to remodel his hotel."

"Is that the same Dr. X.?"

"One and the same."

"Didn't he tell you anything about his project?"

Loos nods anxiously. "Well, yes he did, but I will not be able to work for him; I know we will not get along!"

"Why not, Dolfi?"

Loos sulkily shrugs his shoulders.

"But Dolfi, you could earn a lot of money, the debt could be deducted from that, and we could use the rest to take a trip to France!"

Loos is still upset. Money doesn't interest him, but he would like to take a trip to France. "Alright then," he says finally, "I will take the job, but I will tell you one thing, Lerle, if Dr. X. ever tries to force me to do something I do not want to, we are leaving immediately, Lerle!"

I promise that we will.

The first meeting goes fairly well. Herr Dr. X. kills me with his fierce looks, he threatens me that that I will have to pay for a lost season if the construction is not completed on time, but otherwise everything goes quite smoothly.

Loos inspects the building. As usual, the basic plan is drawn up within five minutes, here an opening will be made, there a wall removed, from these two dark chambers one large room constructed, and so on. Dr. X. nods with enthusiasm. He is swept along by the tempo, by the quick practical thinking of this man, mesmerized. He is a very intelligent man and I cannot understand my husband's misgivings!

Dr. X. invites us for tea at his apartment. The sitting room is furnished in dark mahogany and the walls, too, are paneled in mahogany, the curtains are dark. "Here, this is my favorite room," says Dr. X. contentedly. "I know, Loos, that this room is in keeping with your style."

"With my style? Dear doctor, this is not a living room, this is a crypt!" Icy silence. The master of the house, peeved, lights himself a cigarette and says defiantly:

"I cannot stand those modern colourful things," then, resuming, "You do work a lot with mahogany, with dark subdued colours …"

Loos shakes his head. "Since my stay in Paris, that has fundamentally changed. I love bright colours. My most recent and most favorite dining room is quite colourful. Green, black, red, silver, highly polished – cheap softwoods! My best work!"

Dr. X anxiously: "Well, I would still prefer dark subdued colours in my building. Preferably mahogany."

Loos has lost himself in reverie for a few seconds and is not paying attention. Suddenly: "I have a splendid idea for you, Herr Doctor! We will panel the lobby in blue lapis lazuli. Blue lapis lazuli, it will look fabulous!"

Shocked, the doctor drops the cigarette from his hand. "Lapis lazuli? Are you crazy. Loos? That is way too expensive, I am not a millionaire!"

Loos: "It is no more expensive than good marble." (As a matter of fact, once Loos received a brochure; it said it is now possible to cut lapis lazuli extremely thin and to mount it onto plaster of Paris so that it can be used as a wall covering and still not be overly expensive.) Loos undeterred: "It will look fabulous. The Blue Grotto looks like nothing compared to this!"

The doctor angrily: "I would not think of it!"

Loos fantasizing: "People will be streaming here from all over the world just to see this wonder! You will attract a tremendous number of people, Herr Doctor!"

Doctor X. furiously: "I wouldn't think of it, even it were cheaper than paper! I wouldn't think of it! People would think I was very rich and I would have to pay even more taxes. And as soon as they saw the lobby, the guests would not dare ask the price, they would run out. Out of the question, Herr Loos! I will not use any lapis lazuli! It should look simple and comfortable here. I wouldn't think of it!"

Loos calmly: "You are being stupid, doctor, believe me! You will often think back to my words! You do not know what is good and beautiful!" Sarcastically: "I suppose you would prefer that I decorate everything in a rustic peasant style, like the parlor in an old German farmhouse with hearts painted on the wall, that would really be cozy! By the way, you would fit in there very well, Herr Doctor!"

The doctor, snow white: "What am I? I would fit into a farmhouse parlor? I'm going to get another architect! ... I was counting you as one of my friends, but that is really going too far!" He opens the door, I want to say something else, boom, the door is slammed shut behind us.

"Dolfi!"

"I said at the very beginning, Lerle, that I cannot work with that man! Why did you talk me into doing it! Now you see what happens when you don't go along with me!"

We walk, unhappy, back to the hotel. Sighing, I pack, and get everything ready. Loos has lain down on the bed with Kiki lying on his chest. Frau W. comes in. The poor woman pales as she finds out everything. She feels very awkward about the whole story. She is friends with Dr. X … she admires Loos very much. Perplexed, she remains sitting a few minutes. Then a shimmer of hope spreads over her pretty face.

"Please don't leave yet," she says, "I will talk to Dr. X." Three hours later, she comes back out of breath. She is very pale, about to collapse from exhaustion. "I have spoken to Dr. X., it was not easy. In the beginning, he didn't want to hear a single word and almost kicked me out the door. But finally, because he does basically like Loos too, he settled down! He is sorry for having caused such a scene … after all, Dr. X. did find the remodelling plans completely to his liking … The interior decorating is a different matter however! Being an artist, Loos sometimes simply has ideas that a simple man cannot go along with."

Loos, the artist, is now in bed. This time he is really deaf. No, he does not want anything more to do with this man. Now only the threat that he really will have to pay back the 250 dollars and go to Pilsen instead of Paris moves him to take up negotiations again.

The lapis lazuli is not mentioned again! But at night, before falling asleep, he murmurs to himself, "Lapis lazuli … lapis lazuli … lapis lazuli …"

LOOS' IDEA FOR RENEWING THE BONDS OF THE FRENCH-CZECHOSLOVAK ALLIANCE

We learn that the writer Marcel Ray is staying in Prague, accompanied by a French minister. It is impossible for Loos to leave B. to go and see Marcel Ray. He decides to send me immediately on a mission to Prague.

"As soon as you arrive," says Loos, "you are to go to the French embassy in Hradschin. You will present your calling card and ask that they admit you first, ahead of everyone else. You are to tell Marcel Ray the following:

First: I, Adolf Loos, would like to found a school of architecture in Paris. I need funds for this school that I do not have. Ask if the French government would like to do something for me.

Second: I visited Versailles last year. The palace is still in good condition, but the stone pavement in the courtyard in front of the palace has completely deteriorated. Tell Marcel Ray I have the following idea: Czechoslovakia has the cheapest paving stones and an excellent knowledge of how to work with them. I have never seen paving anywhere in the world as beautiful and as original as in Prague. Since people usually do not look up when they are walking but instead down on the ground, an attractive pavement has nowadays almost become more important than the facades of the houses. The French should commission some Czechoslovak pavers to go to Versailles. They should incorporate the French and the Czechoslovak crests into the pavement to commemorate and strengthen the French-Czechoslovak Alliance. It certainly would be a great honor for Czechoslovakia to present France this paving as a gift.

Then tell Marcel Ray that he and the minister should go and look at the house I built in Prague. Understood? Repeat it! Good! … Your train leaves in half an hour."

"Right now?"

"Yes, immediately! Take Kiki along so that you do not feel so lonely."

So Kiki and I travel all night long. In the early morning, the receptionist at the embassy in Hradshin is hardly delighted when a sleepy woman in a gray travelling dress, a dog on her arm, knocks on the door and demands to be let in immediately. Distrustful, he leads her into a white salon with furniture covered in light blue damask. Here she waits many, many hours. Kiki, the dog, has conjured up a large dark stain on the beautiful sofa … Morning sun breaks through the high windows, painting gray frames on the golden, reflective floor. A servant in a red coat with gold trim finally comes in. The double doors open: Marcel Ray.

In a friendly manner he shakes my hand, asks how his friend Loos is doing. He is a man with intelligent, clear features. I make my request. He listens to me smiling, then says:

"To found a Loos School would be an achievement for the youth of today. I will do my very best to see that it will be brought to life. The idea of paving the courtyard at Versailles is original and I like it very much. I will suggest it … To see the house by Loos is my greatest wish. I will go there as soon as possible … Thank you very much!"

That very same day Marcel Ray went with the French minister to the Müller house that Loos built in Prague.

THE MILL RESTAURANT

Loos has a new idea. He wants to turn a small mill near Prague into a place for excursions and a restaurant. Near Paris there are several very elegant places of this kind.

While the guests listen to the cheerful clapping of the mill, champagne is being drunk diligently. Anyone can watch in the kitchen how the joint is being roasted on a spit over a large open fire.

Loos discovers a small mill near Prague, which seems suitable to him. He gets a developer, Dr. Kapsa, interested in the idea, who drives out with us, accompanied by his wife, to inspect the mill.

Loos wants to start out small. The grassy plot in front of the house on the waterfront should be tidied up, a few tables with colourful tablecloths set out. The large courtyard is well suited to park the cars, a dining room for guests can be arranged for rainy weather. The miller is a simple man who is quite willing to provide the place at a low rent.

On the other side of the grass, by the water, is a small overgrown garden. "Here," says Loos, "there will be a little menagerie. A couple of monkeys, exotic birds, and when more money is available, a few more animals will be added."

A wine merchant in Prague is then sought out to supply beverages.

The whole plan falls through in the end though because the road from Prague to the small mill is too difficult for cars. The money to have the road fixed, of course, cannot be found.

AND ALL THE BELLS SHOULD RING

Herr X. comes to us and says the wood paneling is too expensive, he would like to try and get it cheaper. "The carpenter," he says, "is overcharging me. I want to bargain him down."

Loos falls silent. Then he looks his client straight in the eye: "Let me tell you something," he says, "and may all the bells of the city ring this out: Never bargain a worker down! You should never pressure a craftsman into giving you a lower price, the only option left to him is to give you material of a lesser quality or to do sloppy work. Give him rather a little more money than he asks for and you will receive a thousand times better work, he will work with a lot more pleasure because he is being recognized ..."

GENERAL K.'S CASTLE

We are sitting in a coffee house in a small town. An elegant, handsome officer comes rushing over to us. General K. "My dearest friend." He embraces Loos and beams with happiness. "Loos … !"

Dolfi introduces him: "General K. – my wife. See, Lerle, this is the man I have brought misfortune upon. When I was giving my lectures at the Sorbonne in Paris, he was my most assiduous student. I said once back then that the only reason the Germans lost the war was because they marched more slowly than the French. I also thought their laced up boots were not very practical. What did this man do? He returned back home and tried to introduce some innovative changes in the military system based on my ideas. So now they have transferred him to a small town!"

Loos makes an endearingly childlike, wistful face. "That is what happens to my students when they try to implement my ideas."

General K.: "But Loos, your lectures were my greatest experiences! I am proud to be called your student! I am only stationed here temporarily and will be going to L. soon. Why don't you come visit me there sometime? Besides, I would like to remodel my house."

This comment has aroused my business sense. I say; "I am sure next week we will be going to L."

Loos has for some time buried himself in a pile of newspapers. The words "structural changes" have not made the slightest impression on him. After General K. has left, I say; "Dolfi, General K. has a palace, this will make a terrific project for you!" But Loos is reading, he is not receptive at the moment.

A week later, we are having tea at General K.'s. A small group of aristocrats has also been invited. The old structure is simply beautiful! Gobelin tapestries hang on the walls, few, but authentic old pieces of furniture are sensibly placed throughout the room. One's gaze, however, is captured by the magnificent view. Through the giant window one sees blooming trees and the city, dream-like in the light of the setting sun.

Loos cannot tear himself away from the view. The wife of General K. pulls him aside.

"Dear Loos, we would like to remodel this old house and put in modern furnishings."

Loos pales in anger. "Remodel? ... You want to remodel this magnificent house? ... Put in modern furnishings? ... You want to distract the eye from this magnificent view to the interior furnishings, to marble walls and beautiful wood? Don't you see that the very lack of decoration, the profound simplicity of these walls reinforces the impression a hundred times?"

The wife of the general wants to respond.

"Don't touch it!" With that, Loos cuts short any debate. The matter is settled.

We soon leave. At home, I cannot resist saying something. "Dolfi, what you said is all well and good, but there are other rooms besides the great hall that can be altered. I believe Frau K. also wanted a more convenient staircase. People come from all over the world to visit there and would then have seen your rooms."

Loos is sitting buried in a fortress of newspapers. He looks at me annoyed. "If someone wants to find me, he will find me," he says.

LA BOUTIQUE D'ADOLF LOOS

We want to start a business. It will be called "La Boutique d'Adolf Loos." Loos has the following idea: He wants to begin producing a fairly large series of a particular style of stool. Since the stools would be mass-produced, the purchase price would be low. Once a certain amount of the stools has been sold, another object will be mass-produced, like the sugar shaker that Loos found in Paris and which he finds particularly practical and pretty. The pieces left over from each series would be sold later in the actual boutique.

Unfortunately, it turns out that even with mass production such high-quality objects would be too expensive.

I still want to apply for a patent on the stools, which are very original. Loos laughs at me. The model was found in an Egyptian royal tomb.

LOOS AND THE JEWS

Loos said: “The Jews have brought anti-Semitism on themselves by saying: We are the chosen people!”

Loos wants to be best man at the Jewish wedding of a young student. This is not permitted by the Jewish religion, since he is a Catholic. Loos shakes his head in bewilderment. A Jew can be best man at a Christian wedding. Why is it that a Christian cannot be best man at a Jewish wedding?

He said to me once: “I am an anti-Semite. All Christians should marry Jewish women and vice-versa. In 400 years there won’t be any more Jews … I already have my second Jewish wife …”

Many of students of Loos, students who have worked with him for years, are Jews. Loos says: “I would like to have more Christians among my students, if possible a few aristocrats. Aristocrats are born with culture, they would have to be good architects! But when they become poor, they strangely enough become chauffeurs!”

THE DEPARTURE

Loos is itching to take a trip; it is impossible to hold him back. He has to go, just simply has to go! My mother, who is forever mothering, is very worried.

"You will catch your death," she says, because he has a bit of a cold.

"Oh, mother," Loos replies, "That does not matter! Just imagine I were to die here! No, I would not want to cause you such trouble, I rather leave."

Suddenly I am not feeling very well. I go to bed with fever. Loos most lovingly tends to me for two days. As soon as the fever has subsided, he declares:

"Get up, we are leaving at noon!"

My mother expresses new misgivings.

"Alright then," says Loos, "She can stay home – I am leaving!"

"By yourself?" asks mother.

"Oh," says Loos, "at the most, I will take another woman along with me!"

We leave for the station at noon. Loos is beaming, he has gotten his way.

Nürnberg: Dined at the Bratwurstglöckle in the evening … spent half the night strolling through the medieval city!

Frankfurt: Loos visits the wife of Professor Klimt and Professor Baumeister! He takes me to the Jewish quarter, has the temple caretaker show him the old house of the

Rothschild's! We tour the new housing developments! Loos really likes these developments. "They are very well constructed … they could be mine," says Loos.

Mannheim: Platz, the city architect, takes us on a tour through the city. He shows us the Goethe Theater, which Loos particularly likes. He regrets that there is so little time to spend with Loos in Mannheim. A man who knows what he wants, a man who knows who Loos is …!

Heidelberg: "I did not know Heidelberg before," says Loos, "I am so happy to get to know it!"

We stroll along the river, walk up to the castle and dine there in a very beautiful hotel. The spring sun is warm and pleasant. "I would like to come here again during my lifetime," says Loos.

Darmstadt: Loos goes to see a furniture manufacturer the same evening we arrive. He regrets not being able to meet with him. First thing the next morning, before I am up, he goes to the chair factory and orders a few excellent pieces for Czechoslovakia. Before we leave, he takes me to visit the so-called artist colony. The house of Behrens – the necktie pattern artist, as Loos refers to him – brings an amused smile to Loos' lips.

"There are people already today who are laughing with me about these artist colonies … A few years ago, I was the only one! But it will not take long …"

We travel to Stuttgart. A Loos exhibition, lots of pictures, a few wooden models are being shown here in the commercial arts school! Schleicher, a building commissioner and one of Loos' former students, is waiting for us at the station. He is as excited as a child to see Loos again. We settle down in a hotel. First thing the next morning we go to the exhibition. Loos begins to talk while standing in front of a picture from the Kuhner house. He pulls a matchbox out of his pocket:

"You see," he says loudly, "this is modern architecture! The houses of the future will not be constructed out of steel supported concrete that you have to blow up with ecrasite in order to get rid of them – as was the case at the last exhibition in Paris, ... the house of the future is made of wood! Like the little Japanese houses! It has moveable walls! Modern architecture is: Japanese culture plus European tradition!"

A crowd of people has congregated around Loos. More and more people are coming in from the other rooms. Loos becomes more and more animated ... the fire of youth shines in his eyes! Later, he tells me:

"It is impossible for me to give a great speech in front of a single person. The more people are listening to me, the more intense the atmosphere is, the easier it becomes for me to speak. I have never prepared for a speech! Whatever I say is always improvised on the spot. It would be impossible for me to read a speech off a piece of paper!"

Later that very same day, I have to write an express letter to Mitzi: "Dear Mitzi, please send to us here immediately the black drinking glasses that Josef Hoffmann designed."

"What do you want to do with the drinking glasses from

Josef Hoffmann?"

Dolf gets a mischievous look on his face. "I want to give them to the Museum of Tasteless Objects, which is here in Stuttgart, there they will fit right in!"

We travel on to Zürich.

MILAN

A former student of Loos' is expecting us in Milan: De Finetti. But it is someone else who is really responsible for Loos coming here. Elsie Altmann, the charming Viennese dancer and former wife of Loos. That very same evening we go with De Finetti to the theater where she is dancing. Loos asks me to find Elsie backstage and ask her to spend the evening with us after the performance.

She comes, wearing a simple black dress and a black patent leather feather hat that looks wonderful on her.

"How lovely you look, Elsie," Loos says tenderly. "And you are still young and slender. Are you happy?"

Elsie takes a pencil and writes, "I am alone. I have nothing else in the world but my big suitcase. I travel with it all over the wide, wide, world ..."

Dolf's mouth twitches as he reads those words. Then he takes her hand and kisses it. A tear falls on it ...

De Finetti lives with his young wife in a large beautiful apartment house that belongs to his family. The apartment reminds me of home. It is a real Loos apartment. Loos walks through the rooms and nods, satisfied. The floor in the dining room is made of small red tiles. It looks very attractive. Loos studies it carefully. "These decorative tiles keep the room cool," explains De Finetti.

Loos decides to use the same floor in a house that he is supposed to build in Palestine. He is not ashamed to also learn something from his students.

NICE

We have reached Nice, the city of dreams. Loos is as happy as a little boy.

"Lerle," he calls out, "let's go for a ride in a cab and I will show you the city."

"Shouldn't we go to a hotel first?" I say, enviously watching the other travelers who, with their towers of luggage, are instructing chauffeurs to take them to their destination. "I am tired."

"No. The luggage can stay here at the station, we will go and look for accommodation. I am not going to check in at the first best hotel! I am going to prove to you that Nice is not only the most beautiful, but also the cheapest city in the world …"

We drive through the city. The red houses on the Place de la Concorde seem strange to me. I do not like the old casino on the waterfront at all.

Loos laughs. "The Hotel Babylon that I am going to build here on the Promenade des Anglais will definitely be more to your liking!"

"But Dolfi, there is not any space on the Promenade des Anglais!"

"Oh, these houses will simply be torn down."

Looking somewhat closer, I do indeed see a sign on almost every house: "For Sale."

"First thing tomorrow, I want you to go to the real estate agent and get some price quotes. We must not waste any time, we have to be well-prepared for when we find a wealthy financier."

Loos orders the carriage to stop at the Hotel Ruhl. Ten bellboys rush towards me to help me out of the carriage.

"See, it is a good thing we do not have our luggage along," says Loos, "these lads would have carried it in a long time ago."

I get out. "A room, Madame? 100 francs par jour."

"Get back in," says Loos, "that is way too expensive."

We drive on. At the next hotel the same scenario repeats itself, a room here costs 80 francs.

"Keep going," says Loos. "Keep going, keep going!"

Time passes, we have been driving around for two hours now. Loos is getting fresher and livelier by the minute. I, on the other hand, am tired. Astonished Loos has the driver stop.

"Tired, Lerle? Driver, do you perhaps happen to know a good, cheap hotel?"

"Oui, Monsieur!"

It is not exactly by the beach … No bellboys in colourful uniforms run over to us. A fat man, ruddy complexion, in a white apron, bows deeply in front of us: the "patron." We both climb out. The owner himself proudly takes us to a bright, white room. There is a red carpet on the floor and running water. "And the price?"

"35 francs par jour with full pension, Monsieur!"

Loos beams. "We will stay here. Neither in Vienna nor in Prague will you find such a nice, cheap, little hotel – with running water!"

LOOS REBUILDS THE RIVIERA

The days pass in unceasing work. Loos has contacted all the real estate agents who deal with the selling of houses and property. The news that a famous architect wants to buy some land spreads like wildfire among them. Every day friendly agents show up unsolicited and offer property and houses. All of Nice can be had for a cheap price.

"Don't you think, Dolfi, that this cheap hotel makes a bad impression?"

Loos looks at me astonished. "To the contrary, Lerle. Swindlers always live in expensive hotels … I am not a swindler …"

He never tires of looking over property with the agents. Calculations are made, measurements taken, bartering done. Dead tired, but healthy as never before, he returns at lunchtime. I dare once to softly ask a question:

"Dolfi, how can any of this end well? We do not have any money!"

He looks at me disappointed. Defiant, like a child who is about to have his favorite toy taken away, he replies: "How can you spoil the enjoyment I am getting from working on this project by asking that, Lerle! Didn't I tell you we have to be ready for when the rich financier shows up?!" Irritated, he leaves me; soon he has rebuilt the entire Riviera in his head.

I sigh, but he fantasizes, builds and hopes … fantasizes and builds!

BEAU-BEAU

It is Sunday. The house brokers and property salesmen are not around today. We take a hackney-cab and go for a ride. We drive inland for a change. Soon the sea and the city are far behind us. With the wide-open eyes of a child, Loos looks at the blooming fields of wild poppies, the weathered old farmhouses, the peasants, dressed in black, walking towards us. A big ugly dog jumps up barking at our carriage and accompanies us a little way.

"You know," Loos says cheerily, "We should get a dog again."

I have been thinking the whole time that Loos will not give up his search for a dog. I had secretly hoped that he would, for I shudder at the thought of having to get up at five in the morning and all the other unpleasantness I had inherited with Kiki. But Loos is so happy today and in such a good mood that I do not want to spoil anything for him. "Yes, Dolfi, a dog … Maybe we can buy one in Nice."

"Driver," Loos calls out, "you wouldn't happen to know of a dog dealer who has little Japanese dogs?"

"Mais oui monsieur! I know a woman, it isn't at all far from here," he says, pointing with the end of the whip to a village on the horizon, "that is where her house is, monsieur. She has very beautiful dogs."

"Let's go," says Loos. "Driver," he calls concerned and makes him stop again. "Won't the horse get hungry? We have been underway several hours already!"

The driver sets his mind at ease. He has some feed along with him and will feed the horse at Madame Sou's.

We drive on. We are all in a wonderful mood. Loos, because he is looking forward to the dog, I, because Loos is in such a good mood, the driver, because we are going for such a long ride, the horse, because it will soon get something to eat … But Madame Sou's house is not at all that nearby, we drive on for at least an hour. We stop finally in front of a nice very small house with a large yard. Madame Sou is sitting outside in a flowered housecoat. She comes toward us, talking loudly. A number of dogs barking in all different tonalities accompany her. The dogs are very charming, but even she doubts that they are purebreds. She consoles us by saying that purebred dogs would be less intelligent than these ones here, which she is definitely not wrong about.

Loos is disappointed. He is playing with the little ones, but does not say a word about buying. A little blond girl comes out of the house. She curtsies to us. In her arms she is carrying a very small, long-haired, light brown dog. In the middle of his forehead is a white, triangular spot.

"Hand me your dog for a moment," Loos calls out briskly. She does not really want to let go of him. Loos takes the little dog on his lap and scratches him gently. "He is not exactly purebred either," he comments, "his muzzle is too large and his legs are too long. But he definitely has something, this dog. Look, he has eyes like a human being! Do you like him, Lerle?"

I take him. He happily licks my cheeks and gently nuzzles up to me. No, this dog is not deceitful like Kiki, he will not betray me. I like him a lot. We buy Beau-Beau …

The little girl and her mother ride along with us for a whole stretch, and that comforts the child a little. We become friends with Madame Sou immediately. She gives us lots of good advice for Beau-Beau, which we will not follow. She wants to come visit us in Nice. We say good-bye. The little girl takes a large, checked handkerchief out of her pocket and waves as the carriage finally rolls on again.

Loos waves his gray hat. He is still waving it long after the two have disappeared behind the next crossing.

A FINANCIER APPEARS AND DISAPPEARS

It is the height of the tourist season. The entire city takes on a vibrant appearance. The Promenade des Anglais is packed with people. You see the same people here that you meet in Karlsbad, in Vienna on the Kärntnerstrasse and in St. Moritz.

Loos, lost in thought, stares at the sea, the dog and the people. A short, heavy-set man and a blond woman give us a friendly wave. Loos becomes lively. "Quick, Lerle, go and get him, this is the man I am looking for!"

I edge my way through the crowd. It is in vain, it seems the ground has swallowed the two of them. Loos is very agitated. "This man is one of the most enterprising people of our times. He would have understanding for my projects. He has the money, the connections, and the potential to build. I would also give him the good advice, which he will never regret, to build here and not in Berlin. Nice is still a city with a future for a lot of people ... This man could understand me!"

"Dolfi, who is that man?"

"Herr von L. from Berlin."

Despite diligent searching we do not meet him again. He had been staying at the Hotel Ruhl. Loos writes him a letter; the reply comes from Rome. Herr von L. has received the letter. He finds the projects very interesting, but it does not seem to him profitable enough to build in Nice. Otherwise he would be happy to be of service. Loos disappointed puts the letter aside.

September 1934. I am sitting with Herr von L., who is now

in the business of buying European factories for China, in the foyer of the Hotel Alcron in Prague. We chat.

"I never was a great fan of Loos," he says resolutely, "but he was right back then with his idea of building in Nice instead of in Berlin."

VISIT TO A CEMETERY

The cemetery of Nice is situated high above the city. We drive up the hill on the gentle road. The sky is a deep blue, the sea a deep blue. Loos was not exaggerating. I have never seen such beautiful grounds. The graves are not crowded close together, there are no high walls to obstruct the view. The tombstones stand, bright and peaceful, in the sun – the hill has a gentle slope – they overlook the sea.

Loos walks seriously and slowly down the wide gravel path and looks thoughtfully at the gravestones and inscriptions. He remains standing in front of one grave for a long time. On the stone is written: "God picked an unopened rosebud. In His mercy he wanted to spare her the suffering of life. F. L., eighteen years of age." Loos raises his arms: "If I die in Nice, I would like to be buried here. There is such a beautiful view of the sea from here!"

I have become impatient by now. Annoyed, I pull on his coat. "Dolfi, come, the driver has been waiting so long already. Come on now!"

But he does not leave just yet. "Promise me, Lerle, that I will not be cremated when I die. A dead body is fertile humus. Nothing in the world should be wasted …"

DEPARTURE FROM NICE

One day, Madame Sou actually does come to visit us. Over her pinned up curls she is wearing a large black straw hat with floppy cornflowers on it. Madame Sou finds that Beau-Beau is not in the best shape and that he is very nervous.

"You are not feeding him meat by any chance, are you?" she asks suspiciously.

Loos nods. "But of course!"

"Oh, monsieur," Madame Sou moans, "he is too small, he needs to eat rice, not meat!"

But Loos pounds excitedly on the table. "Madame," he says, "Count Thun in Vienna, who is a first-class specialist in animal care, always gives his dogs meat. A dog is a carnivorous animal. Wild dogs eat only meat."

Madame Sou, who doesn't know who Count Thun in Vienna is, moans unhappily. "Beau-Beau is not a wild dog," she says, "poor little Beau-Beau!" She leaves soon afterwards. She gives us one more piece of advice, which we do follow. Beau-Beau should not be taken along to all the coffee houses, it will not do him any harm if he stays home sometimes and sleeps.

And so we leave him at home and go out to a coffee house. We take a stroll, it gets late. It is after nine o'clock when we come home. The hotel owner is waiting for us in front of the hotel. His red face is even redder than usual. He rushes towards me without greeting us.

"You must leave our hotel, Madame! I have been to your

room. Oh, you did not tell me you had a dog! Oh, you are not allowed to have dogs here … My entire, beautiful room, ruined!"

"What happened?" asks Loos. "Why is the owner so red in the face?"

We have to move out because of Beau-Beau," I reply, "dogs are not allowed here."

"Sir, you dare to insult my dog?! It does not say anywhere that dogs are not allowed here! Why do you only tell us that now?! You do not know at all how to appreciate a guest like me! See here, it is written in all the French newspapers that I am staying at your hotel," and he hands the astonished owner a newspaper that does indeed say: 'Adolf Loos in Nice, staying at Hotel N.' "No one has ever given you such advertising!"

With that, Loos grabs me and we majestically climb the stairs. In our room there is wild chaos. On the floor are some neat little piles and damp spots. The turned-down bedcovers have been pulled onto the floor, dirty and torn. In the middle of this wildness, lies Beau-Beau, the offender, asleep.

Dolfi whispers to me: "Lerle, Lerle, the owner was right. For 35 francs a day with full board one really can't be allowed to do something like this. There is nothing left to salvage. Pack, we are leaving immediately. Give a princely tip!"

An hour later, we are sitting together with the offender in the car. We drive to the best, most beautiful, most expensive hotel on the Riviera, the Hotel Cap d'Antibes on the Cap d'Antibes.

ARRIVAL AT THE HOTEL CAP D'ANTIBES

The arrival at the Hotel Cap d'Antibes is like a fairy tale. Uniformed servants await the approaching car. Our luggage is swiftly unloaded. Like some long-awaited royal couple we stride though the foyer. Left and right the personnel bow deeply. Behind us, his tail held high, marches Beau-Beau, the dog. Everything is festively lit up …

"A room with a bath please!" As Loos writes his name, the doorman gives a start and then bows deeply.

"What an honor!" he says melodiously, "the great architect from Vienna." The owner walks toward us with open arms. He himself takes us to our suite.

"We have a dog along; that is permitted here, isn't it?"

"But of course," says the owner loudly. With lively gestures, he assures us what a pleasure the presence of Beau-Beau gives him.

"See, Beau-Beau," Loos says, beaming, "this is the right hotel for you!"

The door closes. We are alone.

"It is beautiful here!" I whisper.

Loos cheerfully rubs his hands together. "See, Lerle, didn't I tell you from the start, life with a dog is quite something else? Without Beau-Beau we never would have come here!"

JOSEPH ROTH

We are sitting over a cup of black coffee after an opulent dinner. Suddenly, Loos points out a young man to me who is speaking energetically amid a group of Americans. He is slender, blond, and has his lightly wavy hair with a parting to the side. His face is very likable. Intelligent eyes, a slender, curved nose, a fine and somewhat melancholic mouth.

"That is Joseph Roth, Lerle. Go over and tell him I would like to meet him."

I really hate it when he gives me such orders. But Loos is opposed to any kind of superfluous social convention. He would talk to the man himself, but his deafness prevents him from doing that. I get up. I desperately glance around, trying to find a waiter who could do the task for me, but, like in any large hotel, there is never one there when you need him. I take advantage of an opportunity to speak to Joseph Roth as he goes to fetch an ashtray from a table nearby. My shyness immediately turns into arrogance.

"Herr Roth," I say, "Adolf Loos, whose name I am sure you are familiar with, would like to meet you."

Joseph Roth looks at me astonished and amused. "Adolf Loos? Is he here? Of course I know him, indeed, I know him personally, from Paris." As he notices my embarrassment, he then adds, smiling: "Of course there were so many other people there ... he has probably forgotten about it."

Joseph Roth comes over to our table. We are sitting in the

bright, light room of the hotel that looks so much like a castle. The double doors opening out to the sun-drenched terrace are wide open. Steps lead down to the broad, blinding-white gravel path, which, sharply dividing the lawn into two deep green parts, drops straight to the sea. Water and sky blend, blue in blue.

"Are you working right now?" asks Loos.

Joseph Roth nods. "I am writing a new novel, 'Radetzky March', that takes place in pre-war Vienna."

"Are you going to be staying here very much longer?"

"I do not know exactly. I always have to be in the right surroundings for my work. As soon as my novel is finished, I'll be leaving from here."

Suddenly, I realize what the castle and the scenery here remind me of. The emperor's palace in Vienna, Schönbrunn.

I see Joseph Roth again. We have tea together. Joseph Roth looks at me contemplatively and says:

"Forgive me for the indiscrete question. But isn't it hard for you to live with a man who is so much older than you and deaf?"

It is strange, I am asked this question so often. As if other, younger, men do not have quite different flaws! I answer, patiently and truthfully:

"No, it is not difficult, because everything that I am, that I know and that I can do, I have learned from Loos. It has been said, that Loos has always had pretty wives. It is my opinion that the women became more beautiful by being with Loos and because of Loos. I am very happy!"

Joseph Roth looks at me smiling and remains silent.

REMARQUE

Whenever we arrive at a new place, at a new hotel, Loos is always sure to be given the guest book. We are sitting in the dining room, our dinner is finished, Loos is leafing through the guest book. He reads, turns a few more pages, gently shakes his head and says:

"No Czechoslovaks have ever stayed here except for us. Nothing but Englishmen, Americans, a few Frenchmen and Germans. Remarque, the writer, is also staying here. Garçon," he calls, "do you know the writer, Remarque?"

"Mais oui, monsieur, he is sitting over there with his wife."

It is hard to know what to do. Seated at the table in the corner are three gentlemen and a lady. Loos carefully eyes the group.

"Lerle," he says merrily, "make a guess! Which of the three, in your opinion, is Remarque?"

I think about it for a moment. "That is the one!" I point to a blond man with a high forehead and a sharp, bold nose, who is speaking animatedly with Frau Remarque. And then, somewhat uncertain: "Or do you think it is the pale one with the dark artistic curls, gazing dreamily into his compote?" The third man does not seem a likely candidate to me. His hair is dark blond, combed straight back, his face slender and very young, an average-looking face. His voice, however, sounds clear and to the point. I cannot understand any words.

"Well, Lerle?" I shrug my shoulders helplessly. The blond with the hooked nose or the brunette? I do not know.

Loos disappointed shakes his head. "Artistic curls, velvet collars and an animated bearing have nothing to do with art. Only artists that are not really artists resort to such gimmicks. That modest young man there with the clear youthful face will be Remarque." And so it was!

DEPARTURE FROM CAP D'ANTIBES

The Hotel Cap d'Antibes is starting to empty. Joseph Roth has left, Remarque too, and most of the Americans and Dutch. Only a few French, whom we do not know, remain. Some of the locals do come for afternoon teas in the charming pavilion down by the beach ... but Loos is bored. Even the wonderful pool at the base of the red cliffs that belongs to the hotel cannot cheer him up. He needs work and people around him. We are told that Bernhard Shaw, who often spends time here in the summer, will undoubtedly be arriving soon. But Loos does not feel like waiting, he needs a change, he wants to leave.

Then something happens that postpones our departure: The owner of the hotel wants to remodel the hotel and asks Loos to make a plan for him. Loos does not think about leaving anymore. He excitedly paces off the property early in the morning. He writes a letter to Kurt Unger, his student, and asks him to come to us. There are long discussions with the owner of the hotel.

Loos, who likes the site of the hotel, does not want to change its castle-like character. He wants to make an addition on the left and right so that the guests do not have to dine down in the pavilion as was often the case up to now when there were lots of guests present. He wants to enlarge the foyer. Suddenly he is again lively and young, which he has not been in a long time.

But some family incident – I believe the brother of the hotel owner had passed away – takes him away from this construction project. All at once he declares that he does not want to build right now. He asks Loos for an invoice, which Loos indignantly refuses. He does not want money, he wants to build. The owner decides then to reduce our hotel bill to the minimum. This gesture puts Loos in a better mood again. He thanks him exclaiming over and over again, that he has never been to a more beautiful hotel with such a distinguished, select clientele as he found here. Still, he cannot be talked into staying.

We leave. We do not go far. The car takes us that same evening over a winding road, which stretches before us like a shining silver band along the water, to Juan les Pins.

Sequel: A few days later, we are lying, as usual, in lounge chairs on the beach. A young man, pale and tired, is moving slowly from chair to chair, from table to table.

Finally, he walks quickly toward us, breathing a sigh of relief. It is Kurt Unger, whom we had long since forgotten about.

"And how did you actually find us?" asks Loos, curious, after he has ordered the poor lad something to drink, after all we had not left our new address behind anywhere.

"I went back again to Nice from the Hotel Cap d'Antibes. In a restroom there, I saw a notice in a newspaper that read: 'Adolf Loos staying at Hotel N. in Nice.' But no one could give me any information at the Hotel N. either. The owner was not very nice to me at all."

"I can believe that," laughs Loos. "And how did you manage to find your way here?"

"Yes, well," says Kurt Unger, "I thought to myself, Juan les Pins is the only place where anything is happening right now. The other Riviera towns are almost empty. So I came here, hoping that I would find you."

"Bravo!" calls out Loos. "You are a thinking man. Bravo! You will make an excellent architect. Because a good architect must, above all, be able to think logically. You have to stay with us. Besides, it won't hurt you to learn to eat bouillabaisse. It's only fitting."

THE PINE TREES

We are strolling through Juan les Pins. "Where are the pine trees, les pins?" asks Loos, continuing along the coast. We walk through the little town. "Where are the pines?" complains Loos.

We stop a local man. "Tell me," Loos asks the Frenchman, "where are the pine trees of Juan les Pins?"

"Well," says the Frenchman, helplessly shrugging his shoulders, "a couple of years ago there was a whole pine tree forest here, but then they discovered the beach –, the whole coast is rocky. They started building. The village got more visitors, hotels were needed, the trees were cut down, the land divided into lots, houses built."

"That's a pity," says Loos. "What a pity! One could have built and still spared the trees. That's a pity, really a pity!" He sadly looks at the ugly row of houses for which the trees had to be sacrificed.

"But now Juan les Pins is the most visited place around here," says the Frenchman, "money is coming in, and that's the main thing!"

I do not translate those words for my husband, because I am afraid of a burst of fury.

A few days later, Loos discovers a piece of property on which several magnificent pine trees are standing. Loos sends Kurt Unger out to find out what is supposed to happen with this piece of land. Kurt Unger reports back that the owner has the intention of building a small apartment house here.

Loos buys a drafting board and a ruler and is very busy for eight days. He drafts a plan. He works feverishly. "The pine tress, the pine trees," he exclaims over and over again, "must be saved!"

The project was immediately written up in a small article in a French newspaper. The house has a large round entrance gate which is so tall that the pine trees standing inside, in the middle of the courtyard, can be see from far away. The pine trees have been saved!

Loos is happy that he does not have to eat at one particular hotel but instead can go wherever he pleases. Everyday he comes back beaming:

"Lerle, today I have discovered another hotel, the daily special costs only 9 francs. Let's go there." Only coach drivers and locals eat there. We all get stomach upsets. But the next day, Loos comes back again with a new restaurant. He loves the Provençal earthenware, he loves the colourful tablecloths. He says:

"A time will come when everyone will be using earthenware. People will sit at bare tables or at ones covered with bright tablecloths, the restaurant owner in shirt-sleeves will write the price of the food in chalk on a blackboard. That is what the future restaurant business will look like. Cabbies and aristocrats will sit together at one table and everyone will be satisfied ..." Every day an acquaintance or a stranger is brought over for lunch.

Loos tells amusing stories to entertain us. One of these true stories is the following. "Once, in Paris, I was assigned the task of guiding a group of foreigners, of the kind that show up in packs there. I took them to a genuine small French restaurant, where foreigners otherwise never go. The owner set a bowl of small fish on the table as hors d'oeuvres. 'What's this?' asks one. He fishes out, with his fingers wide apart, a fish, holds it up, then lets it glide vertically into his mouth.

'Na,' he said, 'that, I do not like.' The next one follows his example, also fishes out a small fish from the oil, slurps it up loudly and also says: 'Na, that doesn't taste good.' Everyone else in the group does the same. The bill comes. Surprise: everyone has to pay one franc for the hors d'oeuvres! It comes as quite a shock. They all have to pay the same, whether they ate one fish or ten. Somehow that does not want to sink in, worse than that, however, was the singing that the good old boys started up after dinner. And since a couple of Tyroleans were also there, a lot of yodeling went on. Shocked, the owner rushes over to Loos. 'Monsieur,' he asks, 'what kind of a wild bunch of people are these?' 'Wild bunch? These are my fellow countrymen, mein Herr … Austrians …'"

REJECTS

Loos receives a letter from the furniture store S. in Berlin. S. asks Loos to design a dining room for his exhibition in Cologne, to be built precisely according to his specifications and then exhibited there. Loos designs a dining room in black-red-green colours and incorporates softwoods and lacquer finishes which give it a Japanese look.

Coffee and tea services and dinnerware are also to be shown at this exhibition. Loos designs some drinking glasses following the famous Napoleon pattern. He wants to send Provençal earthenware as dinnerware for the exhibit. Harder-working than ever, he visits new restaurants daily, and looks at the dishes. In a little-frequented restaurant, Loos finds some earthenware that pleases him very much. The next day is a holiday. Despite this, Loos drives to a little village near Cannes, where the manufacturer of the earthenware is supposed to be.

To regain strength, in Cannes we each drink a tiny glass of schnapps. Then we take a car and drive up into the mountains. The road is bumpy and takes us past flowering shrubs. High up is a little village. Here, earthenware is produced in every other house. Plates and clay jugs in bright colours are exhibited everywhere in the window displays. Loos rings the doorbell of a small, low-built house.

We are in luck, the owner is home. He takes us into a backroom where there is earthenware in all colours, huge

Provençal water jugs and flower vases. Loos looks around. He takes a soup plate down from a shelf, looks it over carefully and sets it down in front of him.

The owner is very alarmed. "Excuse me, monsieur," he says, "but that is a reject!" Embarrassed, he grabs the plate away from Loos.

Loos looks at him and laughs. "This plate is especially beautiful. I would like twelve soup plates just like this one."

"But it was by accident that the brown colour ran into the yellow," says the proprietor in despair, "that definitely will not happen on those twelve plates!"

"This accident," says Loos, "is very pretty. It doesn't matter at all if the colour is not perfectly uniform. Make me twelve reject plates ... just like this one."

We go for a walk along the shore. Loos is wearing a funny-looking Japanese straw hat of the type now fashionable for ladies. A young, fifteen-year-old girl runs up to us:

"Oh, please, Mr. Chaplin, your autograph!"

Loos, who does not hear, takes the pen she offers and boldly writes "Adolf Loos."

The girl stands still a moment, surprised. "Then you are the great architect from Vienna?" And, after I nod: "That is terrific!"

"What did the little girl say?"

"She thought you were Chaplin."

Two days later is the gala showing of a Chaplin film. We share a private box with Countess T. Loos is wearing a dinner jacket.

"Bravo Chaplin!" a few people shout. Roses fly into our box. A little distance away sits an elegant, gray-haired young man with a slender, intelligent face. It is Chaplin. He looks over to us and laughs.

"Lerle, I have to meet Chaplin! I have a terrific film idea for him."

Loos knows that Chaplin is very reserved. He does not want to overwhelm him and so writes a letter to a common friend, the writer Hollriegel, in Vienna. In the meantime, Loos is pleased to see Chaplin at the beach everyday. He often says in reproach to an acquaintance: "Chaplin just turned around again to look at us. You really ought to wear a pair of trousers that has a less baggy bottom. I am sure Chaplin will copy you in his next film and wear your baggy trousers!"

Hollriegel sends no reply. Loos sighs. "Hopefully Chaplin won't leave before I have had a chance to talk to him. My film idea is this: Years ago when I was in America, I went to eat at a buffet, but I did not have more than 10 cents in my pocket. In America they have large bowls filled with compote; for 10 cents, you can eat as much as you want. You pay when you leave. As bad luck would have it, my 10 cents fall into the compote. I try desperately to fish it out with the big spoon, but it is no use. And so I eat and eat under the scathing glare of the owner until the bowl is empty and I have retrieved my money. Based on this true story Chaplin could make a terrific comedy. The guests watching in amazement, the owner wants to take the container away from him, he fights him, his desperation, his fear, the searching with the big spoon ... All of that would be an idea for a film for Chaplin."

The letter from Hollriegel finally comes, but too late. Chaplin has already left.

KOKOSCHKA IS NO BOCHE

One day, Loos gets hold of a newspaper in which a French critic has written an unfavorable critique of Kokoschka. He talks about his big exhibition in Paris. Among other things, he calls Kokoschka a "Boche." Loos, who considers Kokoschka a great painter of our times, is beside himself. After brief consideration, he writes to the editor the following letter:

"Dear Herr Editor!

I would like to point out to you that your article about Kokoschka is inaccurate. The description 'Boche' alone proves this. Even a child can see that the name Kokoschka is not native to Germany. It is that of a Czechoslovak family, which, like so many, later moved to Austria. One of his relatives is even a Czechoslovak general. I thought you should be made aware of this fundamental error."

Loos sends me with this letter to Henri Matisse with the request that he sign it. I travel to Nice that very same day. Henri Matisse lives in a little house not far from the flower market. A plain-looking woman opens the door and leads me into a bright and furnished bourgeois room. Henri Matisse, a friendly man with a white beard, invites me to sit down. The little room is flooded with sunlight. A canary at the window softly sings its tune. Henri Matisse reads the letter; his face looks infinitely kind. With a little smile he hands it back to me.

"Adolf Loos," he says, "is always the same, ready to fight and to sacrifice himself when someone else's honor is at stake.

His country, the whole world, can be proud of this man. As far as the critic is concerned, it is really almost an honor to be torn apart by him. All great artists of any stature and renown have been terribly criticized by him! Tell Master Loos that and send him my best regards …"

"Did Matisse sign it?" asks Loos, without paying any attention to anything else Matisse said. "Did he sign?" When I tell him no, he looks at me angrily. "Well then, Lerle, I'll just have to send the letter by myself."

And so he did too.

UISTITI…

A boy, about sixteen years old, walks along the beach with a cage in his hand. A lot of children are following him, crowding around him to take a look in the cage.

Loos jumps up from his lounge chair and beckons to the boy. He comes over to us, followed by the flock of children and a couple of adults too. There are two very tiny monkeys in the cage chattering in high pitch childlike voices. They adeptly do acrobatics on a pole, pausing now and then to look, startled, with their old man eyes at the audience.

"Oh, Lerle, those are Uistiti monkeys," Loos exclaims. "They are charming little animals. I had a pair of such monkeys once years ago. We would let the little monkeys run free during the daytime, they liked to climb around in the trees and would always come back home again in the evening. One day the female caught cold and, despite the most loving care, she died after a few days. The male monkey would not touch any more food after that! He crouched down beside the empty cage. Then something strange happened. I had never thought that such a thing was possible with animals. He climbed up onto the roof and, stiff, let himself fall onto the street. He broke his neck and was dead … he had committed suicide!"

PRINCESS LICHNOWSKY

Princess Lichnowsky had sent her congratulations to Loos, whom she had never met, on his sixtieth birthday.

Loos wants to meet her in person. "I would like to see the woman," he says to me, "who has written a book that expresses my own innermost thoughts and feelings. I could have written 'The Battle with the Specialist'."

The princess is just as delighted to get to know Loos. A horse-drawn carriage takes us to her beautiful villa. A livery servant with white gloves opens the door. The princess, a tall, blond woman with fine but sharp features, walks quickly toward us.

"I am so glad you have come, dear Loos!" she says cordially. We have tea on the terrace with a view of the sea. Next to the princess sits Lurch, a thin gray dog who suspiciously sniffs at our Beau-Beau. Lurch is the hero of her last novel, 'On the Leash'.

A lively conversation is soon in full swing. The princess and Loos are very similar in the way they look at the world. I also find a resemblance between them in their physical appearance.

After tea, the princess takes us into a fairy tale garden. An American millionaire, now living in Japan, had it designed. Narrow winding paths lead up a low rise that softly descends into the sea. Here a grove of orange and lemon trees has been planted. There are also wonderful trees from foreign lands,

Japanese bonsai trees and exotic flowers. Loos shows little interest. What he admires most is a tree with golden yellow trumpet blossoms, which are so-called because each blossom resembles a swinging, yellow, mail coach horn. He devotes his attention however, to Lurch, the novel hero, and a small, charming, brown dachshund.

We stay until evening falls, and affectionately say goodbye. In return for her kindness, Loos sends the princess a large, golden-yellow Provençal jug of honey, the type sold by the local peasants.

HOW LOOS GETS A PROJECT AND A PORTRAIT

A lady and a gentleman walk in. The lady is very pretty, redheaded with dark eyes. "W. X." mutters the gentleman, a tall slender man.

"We read in the newspaper that you were here, Herr Loos," he says, "and since I am Viennese too, I wanted to come and see you."

"Pleased to meet you! Is your wife Viennese too?"

"My wife is French; she does not understand much German."

"That is too bad," says Loos. "Do you speak English? Unfortunately, I do not speak French," he adds, smiling.

W. X. is a sculptor. He asks Loos to sit for him for a portrait. Loos cordially agrees. We now get together with the young couple fairly often. They are living in a charming little apartment in Nice. In the living room they have put down gray linen with cherry red borders, which covers the floor up to the walls.

Whilst Loos sits for the portrait, we prepare lunch in the tiny kitchen adjacent to the living room. Sometimes we also go for a swim down at the beach.

One day W. X. brings some house plans with him. One of his relatives owns a magnificent villa on the Promenade des Anglais. To rent out such a villa is difficult, to sell it impossible. He would like to make use of this villa somehow.

Loos immediately takes a trip to Nice to see the villa. He likes it very much indeed. He does not want to change anything; he always has respect for the work of a colleague whom he admires. But he does have a wonderful idea: the villa is not situated directly on the street, there is a garden in front of it. Loos would like to extend the lowest terrace out to the edge of the street.

"There is room here for a nice coffee house," he says. He also adapts part of the inner hall for this purpose, the remainder of the villa could be rented out. Since the terrace is somewhat elevated, rooms can be created beneath it, which, although partially subterranean, could be used in the evenings or in the event it rained. The owner has the plans sent to him but hesitates to have them carried out. When asked what he owes Loos, he replies, "10 percent if and when you have it built, and one cup of free coffee every day thereafter!" He is especially looking forward to the coffee.

The portrait of Loos is nearing completion.

"I think I'll have it cast in bronze," says W. X. "It will be more impressive in bronze."

"If the portrait is good, the material does not matter," grumbles Loos. "Why bronze? That is way too expensive!"

"I can certainly let you have it for less money if it is in plaster," says the artist.

"What did you say? Let me have it? Did I ever tell you I would want you to let me have it? And for less money? You are asking me for money?! You should pay me something for sitting for you. Very few people have been granted that honor, my dear sir!"

Only the repeated assurance that it was all a misunderstanding calms Loos down. A picture of the portrait was published later on in the Prager Presse. I do not know what happened to it. After that, I did not hear anything more from W. X. and his charming wife.

LOOS AND BEAU-BEAU

Beau-Beau is ill. The most lovable of all dogs stares at his master with big sad eyes. He drags himself around painfully. Loos gets a cab and we drive to the veterinarian.

"Well," he says after the examination, "he probably ate something bad. Don't let him run around free and only give him rice to eat."

"Poor dog," says Loos sadly.

We drive back. Beau-Beau cowers either on the lap of his master or under his seat. He completely ignores me. The weather is wonderful for bathing. I swim far out. Who do I see running toward me with his tail wagging and his nose full of sand? Beau-Beau the dog!

"Well, Dolf, why did you let him run free?"

Loos makes a guilty face. "I couldn't stand, Lerle, to watch the dog pining! He wanted to run free … Just see how happy he is now!"

"Yes," I argue, "and now he is eating sand!"

"A dog has more instinct than a human. The sand will cure him!"

A few days later, he has another attack. Loos is miserable. We take a taxi again and drive to the veterinarian.

He makes a very concerned face. "It's the falling sickness," he says, "the dog needs to have shots. He has to stay here. I have a dog sanatorium."

"I am happy to pay more than the usual fee," says Loos.

"But, please, treat him well!"

We drive home, worried. Loos has no peace. He drives out every day to see Beau-Beau.

Our departure is sudden, as always. It is out of question to take Beau-Beau along. But Loos says:

"I simply do not have it in my heart to leave Beau-Beau in the sanatorium. He isn't at all lively anymore, he hardly even wags his tail when we come. That is not the illness, oh no. Beau-Beau is getting melancholic because of his depressing surroundings."

"Couldn't we give him to W. X.?" I ask timidly.

"To W. X.?" Loos is enthusiastic about the idea.

Frau X. loves Beau-Beau like a child. She also has another dog. She will take care of him and love him.

Shortly after our arrival in Paris comes a letter from W. X. Beau-Beau is very sick, he will never be completely well again. Never again! Loos holds his breath for a moment, then writes a telegram: "Have Beau-Beau put to sleep immediately!" – "I love him too much, I want to spare him the suffering! Never be healthy again! I could not bear that thought."

OUR TRIP TO PARIS

Loos is studying the timetables. Never is a trip undertaken without having carefully gone over all possible trains. Loos is the ideal man for organizing a trip. This time, we are travelling back to Paris. Loos finds trains from small local railways that run through the mountains to Lyon.

"I want to get to know the country and the people," he responds to my objection that these trains are probably very uncomfortable.

The trip is uniquely beautiful. Mulberry trees, deciduous forests, unusual flowers grow in the stony ground. The train takes us up, higher and higher. The mountain and the valley remind me of the Semmering area, shepherds with herds of sheep move along the mountain roads.

The train stops at every small station. Peasants and country folk carrying baskets and bags get off and on, chatting animatedly. I can hardly understand them. The language is similar to Italian. The people are dark-eyed and handsome. We are the only foreigners in these trains. A friendly farmer helps me to load and unload our burdensome luggage.

We change trains often. We travel slowly past old farmhouses with large curved gates.

"Here, I want to learn," says Loos. "Only once I know enough about the country, the people, and the customs, which are influenced by the terrain, would I attempt to build here."

A new valley opens in front of us. The stone houses nestled

up against the rocky cliffs seem to be a part of the cliffs themselves.

"And one has to find out what type of building material is cheapest and the easiest to obtain here in order to save money, labor and time."

We spend one night in a small village, the name of which I have forgotten. There are two seats left in the old-fashioned yellow stagecoach that seems to have come straight out of a children's fairy tale book. The inn, sheltered by blooming chestnut trees, is simple and clean.

Loos immediately starts a lengthy conversation with the innkeepers. He soon finds out that one can stay here in the summer for 15 francs a day; also that people from Paris actually do come to stay here. Yes, an omnibus drives three times a week through the mountains to southern France and back to Paris. Loos asks about the price of groceries, some of which have to be brought in from far away because the soil is so rocky here. He asks and asks and the wife of the innkeeper is delighted that this stranger should take such an interest in her life. She willingly provides the information until Loos knows everything, even their private life and habits.

Then, he the never-tiring, orders us each a glass of wine. Sitting beneath the chestnut trees, we watch the children playing on the village square. After taking a short rest, Loos tours the village, studies the old buildings and houses and lingers a while in the church that stands partially in ruin.

Lyon. We spend two hours there, from ten to twelve o'clock

at night. The air of this industrial city is oppressive after all the sunlit fresh air. We stroll through the city, which is not very alive. There are many taverns here. We eat dinner and drink a wonderful glass of beer in a simple lounge.

A blond man who works in a silk factory is happy to give us some information about the city and the people. Loos has him give us a detailed description of silk and its manufacturing. I have the impression that this industrial city does not offer much in the way of intellectual life and is probably quite provincial.

At one o'clock we are already in our sleeping car compartment. The train is almost empty. Loos smiles contentedly.

"See, Lerle, how silly people are! This train, the only one which has second class sleeping cars, is hardly occupied." Loos is really the born travel marshal.

Five o'clock in the morning. The conductor knocks. In a quarter of an hour we will be in Paris. "Ach," murmurs Loos, "that is the end station, the worst that can happen to us is that we will be put off onto a sidetrack." He goes back to sleep. Five minutes before the train is to arrive he leaps out of bed. He is completely changed.

"Lerle," he calls out, "we are arriving in Paris!" Standing in front of the mirror he meticulously knots his tie. And because it does not turn out nice enough, he ties it again. Paris … Paris.

A taxi takes us through the awakening city to Montparnasse. Loos has the driver stop in front of the Café du Dôme.

Our seven suitcases, small trunks and dressing cases are unloaded in front of the Café. Loos sits down at one of the iron tables, smiling contentedly. The old waiter, who knows him, comes happily over to him.

"One oatmeal as usual," Loos orders. Under the table, two drunks are snoring.

LOOS WANTS TO WORK

Loos has come to Paris to work on a project. In the meantime, the client has reconsidered having the remodelling done. Loos is very upset, does not feel well and stays in bed. The suitcases are lying around his bed, we got them from Kniže, where they were kept in storage. They are full of clothes, but moths have nested and destroyed almost everything. Now they are lying around open here. They give off a musty smell.

"Don't throw them away!" the sick man cries. "Those are still my best clothes in there, don't throw them away."

To put him in a better mood, I bring him some chicken and mayonnaise, which he enjoys eating. Then I hurry to the post office. I come back after an hour. Loos is still lying in bed. In his one hand he has the piece of chicken, in the other the paper with mayonnaise; the whole bed is smeared with mayonnaise.

"Read it," he shouts, "read this letter!" A student writes:

> "Herr X. from P. wants me to take charge of a project by myself. Since I am working for you I didn't accept. What should I do?"

I find this letter is very nice and correct.

Loos, on the other hand keeps repeating: "He is stealing my work! He is stealing my work!"

"He is asking you first," I say, agitated, "we can prevent it!"

“Don’t prevent it, don’t prevent it,” cries the sick man. “If the client would prefer to go to the apprentice than to the master it’s his own fault, his own fault! Betrayal! Betrayal,” Loos groans, “and you too, Lerle, you too!”

He pulls a newspaper page from the bed, takes my hand in an iron grip and points to an article. “It says here that the famous actress Lilian Harvey has finally decided to have her villa built in Nice. Didn’t I tell you a hundred times to go and see her? A hundred times, a thousand times! But you are my biggest enemy. You didn’t go. Betrayal! Betrayal! You don’t want me to work, to build ...!”

Suddenly he sits up in bed. His eyes are staring at me, wide-opened and terrible. “Go away!” he screams, “go away, leave me alone! – You will cause me more grief than Josef Hoffmann, my worst enemy! Go away, leave me alone!”

*

I leave. A young painter who we had complained about the day before is standing in front of the building. He gets on my heels and accompanies me. I am so unhappy and so shattered that I hardly even notice him.

Suddenly, a voice next to me says: “Did you know that Loos was much happier and healthier when he lived in Paris without a wife? A wife hinders a person like Loos –, she destroys him. A woman is an enemy for Loos!”

Every word that the stranger says is like the stab of a dagger to me. Were those not my very own thoughts? “And do you think,” I say, shaking, more to myself than to him, “That Loos would be happier if I left him?"

The painter nods. "Absolutely! A genius has to be alone!"

At another time I would have laughed at these words, but now I tremble. The thought of leaving Loos surfaces. But before I carry out this crazy idea, I want to see if the painter is right. I pretend to leave Loos.

Two days later, I see Loos on the arm of his best friend, Oskar Kokoschka, walking through the streets of Paris. His step is lively, he laughs, he is happy …

Many years later, Kokoschka told me: "Back then, Loos came to me in Paris. Tears were pouring from his eyes. He sank, sobbing, into my arms. 'My wife, my wife has left me!'

'Oh go on,' I said to him, 'that's no great loss, there are lots of women in the world!' And I took his arm and shook him. Loos sighed with tears. Then he pulled himself together, lifted his head up high and walked for hours with me through the streets of Paris."

— — — — — — — — — — — — — — —

I am sitting again in a rattling train, but my thoughts are far away – with Loos. No, I do not want to hurt him, I would rather go away … far away.

Weeks go by. I am living in a daydream. Heavy housework keeps me from thinking. A tremendous apathy has settled over me. I must go back and yet I cannot. My hands have no strength, my thoughts are confused. I cannot undertake anything. But I only need to close my eyes and I am with him – with Loos. Whenever I make the effort to try to shake myself out of it, I hear a cold, merciless voice:

"A woman who has left me may never come back again!"

People take me to my homeland. It makes no difference for me where I live. I only have to close my eyes and I am in my real homeland – with Loos!

*

Loos has some business to take care of in P. where I live.

A sympathetic girlfriend asks me: "Don't you want to go to him? Don't you want to see him?"

See? Really? Not with my eyes closed?

My feet can barely carry me up the hotel steps. I am completely numb. Softly, like a thief, I open the door. He is asleep. I go over to him on tiptoes. I kneel down, trembling with happiness.

"Lerle," he whispers, his eyes still closed. "Lerle …" Then he opens his eyes, closes them, opens them, reaches out to touch me. "Lerle," he calls tenderly. Tears are pouring from his eyes. "Lerle, why did you leave me?"

I bury my face in his hands. "Oh, you," I whisper, crying, "let me be with you forever, then everything will be fine! Don't ask! It was insane … completely insane!"

A voice resounds around me. A voice that I have heard a thousand times in my dreams, I am now really hearing:

"A woman who leaves me may not come back!"

I look at him. Tears are still on his cheeks, but his eyes look clear and unmerciful.

What has happened?
Why is it suddenly so dark in me?
All of the lights in my soul have gone out!

— — — — — — — — — — — — — — —

And that was how life with Adolf Loos ended.

SAYING GOOD-BYE

Loos has been placed in the Rosenhügel Sanatorium in Vienna. He suffered a stroke. My only thought is to see him. Finally I am able to get to Vienna. I arrive at the sanatorium, I ask the porter about Loos; he tells me the ward and room number. Next to him stands a beautiful blond woman. "You want to see Loos," she says, "I ought to tell you, he does not recognize anyone anymore. I am his nurse and have my day off today. When I came back from holiday the day before yesterday, he did not recognize me."

"Please, nurse," I say, "take me to Loos." Walking together a short way, I talk to the nurse. "It is strange," she says, "but because Loos reads newspapers everyday despite his illness, I have got into the habit of doing it too, all in all I have learned quite a lot from Loos. The uniform that I'm wearing, for example, I had it made according to his instructions." We stop in front of a pavilion in the garden. "There," she says, pointing to a window. There indeed, standing at the window, is Loos, held up left and right under his arms by doctors. He looks blankly off into space. Suddenly his eyes fall on me, on the nurse, and then back on me. A smile slides quickly over his rigid face. Then he tears an arm loose, points to me and says clearly and plainly: "Lerle." I run into the building, I try to look happy and radiant, he is not supposed to notice that his condition is affecting me. He motions as if making an introduction to the doctors and says, "my wife" then whispers to me a little joking comment. At that moment he is quite his old self again. Then – as it is apparent that speaking is quite a strain for him – he takes a pencil and writes: "Heidelberg, Mannheim, Stuttgart, Zurich. Milan – our trip." Then he points to me, to himself, to the door. He wants to go away, go far away with me, to the south. I help him into a wheelchair and push him out into the garden. He takes my hand and is pleased, he laughs, he is happy. The time passes all too quickly. I have to leave, I let him know that I will come back again soon. Loos looks at me, there is an infinite sadness on his face, he takes both my hands and presses them to his chest. His lips whisper something unintelligible. "Oh, yes, yes, I will certainly come again tomorrow." I nod. But he only slowly shakes his head, as if he knew better. I leave. Down by the gate I stop and look back up to him. He is sitting up straight in the wheelchair, motionless. He does not speak, he does not wave, he looks towards me …

NOTES

In 1931, between March and July, Loos and Claire travelled through Germany, Switzerland, and Italy on their way to the Riviera, before heading back to Paris. They stopped on their way through, or stayed at, Nürnberg, Frankfurt, Mannheim, Heidelberg, Darmstadt, Stuttgart, Zürich, Milan, Nice, Cap d'Antibes, Juan les Pins, Cannes, and on their way to Paris, went through the mountains between the Riviera and Lyon. They arrived in Paris at the Café du Dôme, which had been known since the turn of the century as a gathering place for intellectuals and artists.

Loos and Claire separated in Paris, in 1931.

KEY TO NAMES

* P. (Pages 8, 132, 135) – Pilsen

"A second Kobenzl" (Page 13) – refers to the Hotel Kobenzl in Salzburg.

* "One of my girlfriends, ... who is now working for Loos" (Page 21) – refers to Ilse Günther (von Hennig), who worked with Loos on the commissions for the Tzara, Moller, Khuner, and Müller houses.

* General K. (Pages 23, 81-83) – General Klecanda

* Client B. (Pages 30, 68) – Hans Brummel, Pilsen

* Frau X. (Page 32) – Genia Schwarzwald

* Client X. (Page 43) – Dr. Gustav Scheu

* Pension Z. (Page 50) – Pension Zenz is located on the Alserstrasse in Vienna.

The artist Kolo Moser (Page 52) is Koloman Moser, who founded the Wiener Werkstätte in 1903 with Loos' archrival Josef Hoffmann.

* The big exhibition abroad (Page 64) mentioned in the chapter "I Am A Cosmopolitan" took place at the end of 1930 in Milan.

* Concerning Loos' citizenship (Page 64) – He chose Austrian citizenship after the collapse of the monarchy and did not accept Czechoslovak citizenship until later in life and only then in addition to his Austrian citizenship.

Masaryk (Page 66) – Tomáš Garrigue Masaryk was the founder and first President of Czechoslovakia, who granted Loos a regular government honorarium upon his 60th birthday.

Machar (Page 66) – Czechoslovak poet Josef Svatopluk Machar

Starhemberg (Page 70) – Ernst Rüdiger Camillo Starhemberg, conservative Austrian nationalist politician, who had contact with the early Nazi movement of the 1920's but after Hitler's failed coup d'etat (the Beer Hall Putsch) rejected the movement. As vice chancellor during Vienna's civil war in 1934, Starhemberg fought to keep Austria free from a Nazi takeover.

* Doctor X. (Pages 71–75) – Dr. Oskar Simon was the owner of the Esplanade Sanatorium in Karlsbad that Loos remodelled in 1930/1931.

Hotel Babylon in Nice (Page 91) – Loos designed the hotel in 1923, but it was never built. He took the name from a popular novel by Arnold Bennett, *The Grand Babylon Hotel.* It was to have 1000 beds in 700 hotel rooms, a gigantic building. Loos wrote,

> Each hotel must be designed to meet the needs of its setting. I decided on the Riviera, which I know well. But each hotel ought also to be designed for a particular class of society. Structural shortcomings, however, make this impossible. Dark rooms facing the yard must be let off cheaply even in luxury hotels. A hotel, set back on terracing, however, has no such rooms: it has only front rooms. In addition, by means of girder construction (i.e., by the use of structural steel) the east, west and sunny sides can be elongated. The main thing is that each room has its own terrace. […]
>
> If we compare the project with two linked pyramids, we may speak of two enormous sepulchral vaults. One of these is to be designed as an ice palace, the other as a large ballroom. Between the two there is a large top-lit room which – instead of a glass roof, which would not be a pretty sight from the inner terraces – is to be given a water tank with a Luxfer [prism] floor" (qtd. in Adolf Loos, *Pioneer of Modern Architecture* by Ludwig Münz and Gustav Künstler, 134–136).

Bernhard Shaw (Page 107) is the Irish playwright and author George Bernhard Shaw.

* Furniture store S. (Page 114) – Schurmann Brothers Furniture Store in Berlin

* The exposition mentioned (Page 114) is the 1931 International Interior Decoration Exposition in Cologne.

* Herr W. X. (Page 123) – sculptor Francis Wills

* A picture of the portrait bust of Adolf Loos by Francis Wills (Pages 123-125) was printed in the pictorial supplement of the *Prager Presse* on July 12, 1931. June 1931 is cited in the picture's caption as the date of completion.

*[*Reprinted from the 1985 edition of Adolf Loos Privat, edited by Adolf Opel.]*

The German spellings Claire used for Czechoslovak places have been retained in this edition. Czech names are included below:

Laurenziberg – Petřín
Hradshin – Hradčany
Brunn – Brno
Pilsen – Plzeň
Thomas Bat'a – Tomáš Bat'a

NICKNAMES

Claire is referred to by Loos in his letters as "Klara," "Kläre," "Lerle," and "Lärle," the latter of which may reflect the way he heard her name in his head when he spoke due to his deafness.

Claire called Loos "Dolf" and "Dolfi."

ADOLF LOOS' CIRCLE

Below are brief summaries about the artists and writers in Loos' circle mentioned in Claire's book, which should not be taken as any way representing their complete biographies. [Ed.]

KARL KRAUS (April 28, 1874–June 12, 1936) was a Viennese writer, satirist and publisher of the controversial *Die Fackel [The Torch]* and one of Loos' closest friends. He is best known for his defense of language and indicting hypocrisy in all manner of Viennese and Imperial society, but later was criticized for his uncritical use of anti-Semitic clichés, and for supporting the idea that Austrians should abolish all traces of Hebrew in their German and bring the language closer to a "pure" German. Kraus later began reassessing those positions as Nazis rose to power, and he soon began a scathing critique against German politics. Subsequently his works were banned during the Third Reich. Karl Kraus converted from Judaism to Catholicism in 1911 with Adolf Loos as his sole witness. Kraus was related to Claire Beck Loos by a marriage between his brother Alfred Kraus and Claire's father Otto Beck's cousin Rosa Hirsch.

OSCAR KOKOSCHKA (March 1, 1886–February 22, 1980) was an Austrian painter and close friend of Adolf Loos. It is said that Loos advised all of his clients to buy a Kokoschka painting for their homes, including the Becks, who had a large painting hanging in their dining room. Otto Beck's cousin Wilhelm and his wife Martha Hirsch both commissioned portraits by Kokoschka. Martha, one of his more well-known sitters, was known to dislike Kokoschka's painting of her, entitled "Dreaming Woman" (1909); later Nazis used this painting to vilify Kokoschka citing it as an example of his "degenerate art."

PRINCESS LICHNOWSKY, or Mechthilde Lichnowsky, (March 8, 1879–June 4, 1958) was the granddaughter of Empress Maria Theresa of Austria and wife of Karl Max, Prince Lichnowsky, the German diplomat to England from 1912-1914. Mechthilde Lichnowsky wrote eighteen books, in addition to poetry and works for theatre. Among her literary cohorts was Karl Kraus. During the Second World War she was considered a traitor by the Nazis and suffered her books being burnt; however, she was later considered a Nazi accomplice by the communist Czech government and thus was expelled and all of her family's property seized. One of the books she wrote, mentioned by Claire that Loos himself felt an affinity with, *The Battle with the Specialist,* took on all manner of self-conferred "experts" from train conductors to doctors to people with pompous and obnoxious attitudes.

ERICH MARIA REMARQUE (June 22, 1898–September 25, 1970) was a German writer who authored nearly twenty books. He was conscripted into the German army during World War One and wrote about these experiences in the novel *All Quiet on the Western Front* in 1927 (published in 1929). Later, Remarque's books were banned by the

Nazis and many of his family suffered under their regime. He wrote the following letter to Loos while at the Hotel du Cap D'Antibes in 1931, which Claire kept, and which has been reprinted here with the permission of the Erich Maria Remarque-Friedenszentrum in Osnabrück, Germany. It has been translated by the Friedenszentrum's Thomas Schneider.

> Dear and admired Herr Loos:
> I was shattered by your great work, by the lucidity and beauty of your ideas and by the variety and intensity of your creative power — but more shattered by the fact that stupidity, malice and the average were successful for decades in concealing this work — With the wish to get to know a lot more about you, I am
>
> Yours sincerely,
> Erich Maria Remarque

JOSEPH ROTH (September 2, 1894–May 27, 1939) was a Jewish Austrian journalist and author born in what is now known as the Ukraine. He detailed the paths of the Jewish diaspora in Europe after World War One and the Russian Revolution. The subject of his novel *Radetzky March* is the decline and fall of the Hapsburg Empire.

EMIL LUDWIG (January 25, 1881–September 17, 1948) was a writer and journalist who interviewed many political figures including Stalin and Ataturk. He wrote for the *Wiener Freie Presse* and the *Berliner Tageblatt* and is known for his insightful biographies.

BOHUMIL MARKALOUS (Jaromír John) (April 16, 1882–April 24, 1952) was a Czechoslovak journalist and author who lived in Prague. He published an article in 1924/1925 in *Wohnungkultur [Apartment Culture]* entitled: "Adolf Loos: Man of Our Time." He helped organize the celebration of Loos' sixtieth birthday at the Společenský klub about which Claire writes.

JAN SLIVINSKI (Hans Effenberger) was a writer and bookseller whom Loos visited in Paris. Slivinski's circle of intellectuals included artists and Polish refugees.

MARCEL RAY was a German writer, part of the Berlin circle of Dadaists. While not much biographical information can be easily found about Ray, he was well known for his 1927 book *George Grosz: Peintres et Sculptures,* a monograph.

JOSEF SVATOPLUK MACHAR (Februrary 29, 1864–March 17, 1942) was a Czechoslovak essayist and a leader of the realist movement in poetry. He espoused anti-Austrian views and the emancipation of women. His influence is felt widely in Czechoslovak poetry. Machar wrote a brief letter to Claire on August 19, 1932, reprinted here in the photo appendix, the subject of which remains mysterious.

> Madame,
> I have tried this and that but to no avail. I hope that Dr. Markalous will have more luck. The times are horrible, the so-called crisis is everywhere. I don't know if Herr Doctor Masaryk wanted to do something — our 40-year friendship has gone to pieces.
> A dismal letter, no? But ...
>
> Yours faithfully,
> S. Machar

ARNOLD HÖLLRIEGEL (Richard Arnold Bermann) was an Austrian writer who made his name in Berlin between the two World Wars writing non-fiction and novels, and was on the staff at *Die Stunde [The Hour]* where he wrote arts and travel articles. He went to America in the twenties and befriended Charlie Chaplin. He later became a leader for the German Academy of Arts and Sciences in Exile after Hitler came to power.

LOOS' STUDENTS:

HEINRICH KULKA Loos' student and then later, associate, carried out many of his projects including the duplexes at the Werkbundsiedlung experimental housing project in Vienna, which Claire mentions. He published the first Loos monograph *Adolf Loos: Das Werk des Architekten* in 1931.

ZLADKO NEUMANN One of Loos' most trusted collaborators, a Croatian architect, who also served as proxy on Loos projects.

GIUSEPPE DE FINETTI The sole Italian student of Adolf Loos, credited with shaping contemporary Milan.

KURT UNGER was a student and, later, assistant to Loos. Among the work he did for Loos were plans for Dr. Josef Fleischner's villa in Haifa. He also managed the production of Loos' design work in glass and tableware, and became a financial supporter in Loos' last years.

A BRIEF HISTORY OF *ADOLF LOOS PRIVAT*

The original 1936 edition of *Adolf Loos Privat* by Claire Beck Loos was financed by the Beck family and published by the Johannes-Presse in Vienna, which was connected to Otto Nirenstein's Neue Galerie. It was republished in 1985 following contact between Claire's brother Max Beck and Adolf Opel, a filmmaker, writer, and professor from Vienna who has a great interest in Loos and edited the book. Opel visited Max Beck and his wife Elizabeth (Betty) in Worthing in 1982 and added to the book several of Loos' seminal essays and articles about Loos, as well as unseen pictures from Max's collection, which are printed in the following photo appendix.

Adolf Loos Privat had been relatively unknown until 1982 when Burkhard Rukschcio and Roland Schachel released *Adolf Loos — Leben und Werk,* which summarizes episodes of the book and quotes heavily from it to fill out the last four years of Loos' life. There are also a great number of photos in Rukschcio and Schachel's book of Claire, and of Loos taken by Claire, as well as Loos' love letters to her. All of those documents now reside at the Albertina in Vienna.

BECK FAMILY HISTORY

BY JANET BECK WILSON

Until the early 1980's, the community of Loos scholars were not aware of any surviving descendants of the Beck family. This all changed when my father Max Beck attended an international symposium at the Warburg Institute in London in June 1982, entitled *Britain and Vienna 1900–1938*, which focused on the English influence in the works of Loos and his archrival Josef Hoffmann. From the audience my father made informed comments about Loos and revealed himself to be Loos' former brother-in-law, drawing interest and queries from those present, and later, from people who heard about the event. In a letter to me in 1992, the Director of the Institute Sir Ernest Gombrich recalled, "It is not often that we art historians encounter such an authoritative informant [as Max Beck], and everybody present appreciated the occasion." The Becks and the Hirsches, cousins of my grandfather Otto Beck, were some of Loos' first clients and instrumental in getting Loos his early architectural remodelling work in Pilsen and Prague.

Following the death of my mother in 1988, I inherited my father's papers. These included a letter from the Red Cross dated September 21, 1982 where my father was informed of the tragic fate of his family in the Holocaust. I also came into possession of his brown suitcase where he kept all his family pictures, which he left Prague with in haste in 1939.

Some of these pictures have been reprinted here, including images of Claire, the Becks, and Claire's life with Loos; others come from the archives of my cousin, Charles Paterson (Karl Schanzer).

My father's pictures had remained in his suitcase since he crossed over to England following six months of being detained at the Dutch frontier in 1939; he had escaped Czechoslovakia on a false visa arranged by his brother-in-law Steve Shanzer (Stefan Schanzer) that attested he was a photographer travelling with a press team. My father had originally intended to set up a branch of the nail and wire factory, Richard Hirsch Company, in England; he was one-third partner, inheriting Otto Beck's interest in the firm. But his original sponsors backed out of their guarantee. Finally his refugee application was granted when another English firm, the F.N.P. Manufacturing Company, agreed to take him on as a metalworking employee in a wire drawing process.

We now know more details of Claire and her mother Olga's tragic final circumstances. As Adolf Opel recorded in his introduction to the 1985 edition of *Adolf Loos Privat*, "On October 4, 1939 Claire Loos deposited her notes and documents in the Discount and Credit Bank in Prague. These were confiscated by the Germans as Jewish property. Claire was registered with the Jewish Eldership under the number 26,342. From September 1, 1941 on, she was required to wear the Jewish star." From my research in the *Terezín Memorial Book (Terezinska Pametni Kniha,* Terezinska Iniciativa, Melantrich,

Praha 1995), and confirmed by historian Ivan Margolius, we know Claire and Olga were both forced to move to Terezín (Theresienstadt) from Prague in 1941 and 1942. Claire was assigned number 824 on transport "L" for December 10, 1941; Olga was listed on a transport for July 30, 1942.

From this point, the story was only vaguely known to us until a few years ago when we were finally able to get these last pieces of information. From Terezín Olga and Claire were transported separately to Riga, Latvia, where they were killed upon arrival. Olga was deported to Riga on August 20, 1942. Claire was sent earlier, on January 15, 1942.

You have just read about Claire, and hopefully feel you know her as we have come to through her writing. Understand that her death came quickly, which is only a small consolation. She was shot at point blank range presumably by Nazi *Einsatzgruppen* forces [mobile killing units] and was buried in a mass grave in the Bikernieki forest. She was thirty-seven years old.

The connection between Adolf Loos and Claire was often spoken about when I was a child, but after reading *Adolf Loos — A Private Portrait* I began more research, starting with a visit to Prague and Pilsen in 1994. There I met up with my cousin Charles, who had been adopted out of Europe along with his late sister Doris by Charles and Eileen Paterson in Brisbane, Australia. Charles now lives in Aspen, Colorado. He is an architectural designer, and studied under Frank Lloyd

Wright. At age nine, Charles (Karl), with Doris age eleven, were put on a train by Claire, Olga and Max, fleeing from Czechoslovakia alone to Paris. At the station, Claire slipped her diamond ring onto Doris' finger and said good-bye to them, perhaps foreseeing that what they took with them on their persons would be all they would have to survive.

In 1994 Charles and I tried to trace where our grandparents had lived; it was a very emotional trip. We went to Pilsen and searched for the family's Loos-designed apartment. Doris and Charles lived with their grandmother Olga in the flat for nine months before and during the German occupation. He tells the story that in the middle of the night upon hearing news of the German advance, my father Max, Claire, and Olga fled with the two children in Max's Tatra through a wicked snowstorm to a Prague hotel; but it was to no avail, Charles recalls hearing the sound of the Germans marching, and looking out the window in the morning to see tanks in the street. From his forthcoming memoir *Escape Home*, which tells of these harrowing times in more detail, I quote the following excerpt about our trip back to Pilsen in 1994 and our visit to the site of the former Loos apartment. Charles writes,

> Janet, Fonda and I ascended the grand staircase and on the top floor we knocked on the apartment door. When a lady in a white coat appeared, I handed her a note in Czech that our friend Will Semler — son of Loos clients Hanne and Oskar Semler — had written

out for me. The note said that my grandparents had lived there in 1938. The woman at the door smiled and invited me in. To my shock the apartment was bare, had been divided up with plywood partitions and was being used as a microbiology laboratory. I thanked her but quickly withdrew and could not go in. I was heartsick. It had been an exquisitely furnished place and I was almost in tears when I saw what it had become.

In 1940 when Olga Beck moved to Prague, she was forced to relinquish ownership of the Loos flat. Olga wrote in a letter to her son-in-law Stefan Schanzer on November 15, 1940, "My apartment is being demolished now, and I will have to look for a room. It is not easy to undertake such big changes ... But everything can be survived. It doesn't worry me, just makes more work." Upon her relocation all of the Beck furnishings and artwork were stolen.

Our family's initial contact with Loos scholars in Czechoslovakia came to pass through a fortuitous visit I made to Loos' Villa Müller in Prague in 2005. Upon arriving at the Villa for the 11 a.m. tour, I was amazed at the building. When I explained to the guide that I was the niece of Claire Loos she was quite shocked and wanted to know anything I could tell her. The Villa Müller is such a surprise when you walk into the large sitting room, and for me even more so. There I saw a picture of Claire and Loos taken on the gala occasion of his 60th birthday party, attended by family, friends, clients, and artists. Everyone had been photographed on the same settee I was standing in front of. It brought on a feeling I have never before experienced — I just felt cold, and sad for a moment to think that my aunt Claire, who I never met but feel I know, and Adolf Loos, who I — like my family — much admire, had posed for the camera in that very room.

During the visit I took the name of the curator of the Museum, Maria Szadkowska, and decided to contact her as soon as possible on my return to the UK. When I did, I was again asked if I had any stories of Loos, but I only knew a few things as my father very rarely spoke of his life prior to the war. What I did have, however, were photographs, which I brought with me in June 2006 when I travelled back to the Villa with Lyn Cooper, a close family friend who had known my father and our family history well. Maria was excited to meet us and to have copies of the photos, some of which were of Claire and others of my grandparents, the Becks, and their apartment.

In April 2007 I took another trip to Prague with my husband David. Like me, he was very interested in the Villa but even more so when Maria took us to Pilsen to see how restoration was progressing on the Vogel flat, which was part of the first Loos-designed interior owned by my grandparents Olga and Otto Beck before they moved in 1928. There we met Mr. Brummel, who still has an apartment in Pilsen that Loos designed and which is still in its original state. We were able to have a cup of tea together in his apartment. The interior and furnishings are as Loos had left them, and on the wall the fresco by Robert Aigner that Claire mentions in her book remains preserved.

At this time Maria told me the Museum of Prague was organizing a exhibition of Loos work in the Czech lands during September 2008, so for the fourth year in a row, I went back to the Czech Republic to attend its opening. Again I was able to provide information and family pictures, which have travelled with this exhibition to Italy, to Brno in the Czech Republic, and to London in 2011, upon which occasion we are honoured to present *Adolf Loos — A Private Portrait* to the English-speaking world.

BECK DESCENDANTS FAMILY TREE

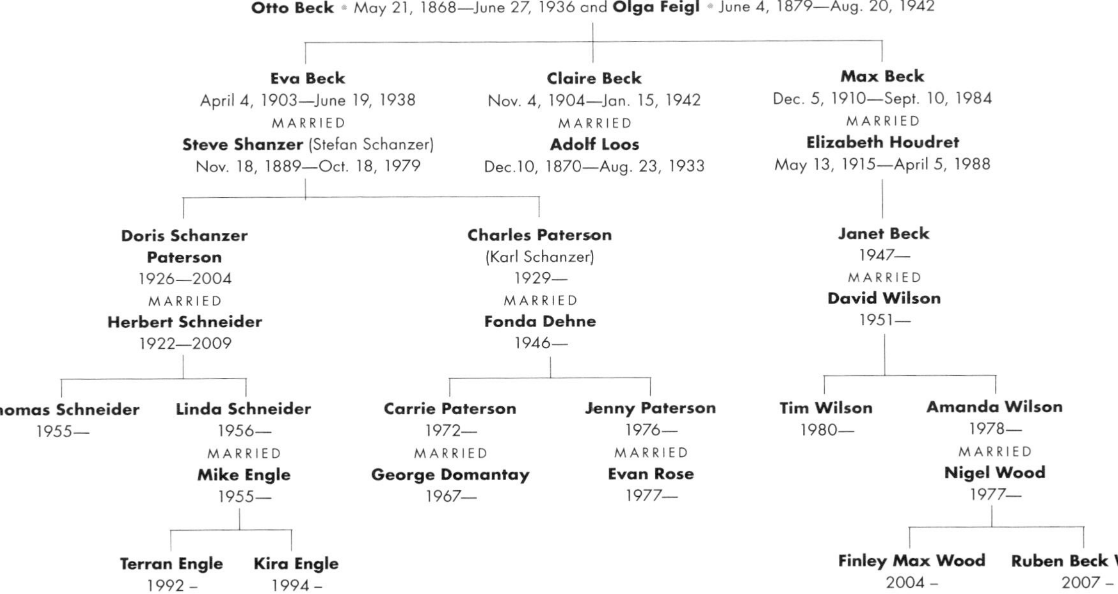

NOTES ON CLAIRE AND LOOS' DIVORCE AND BECK-SCHANZER FAMILY HISTORY

Shortly after Claire left Loos in 1931, her father Otto Beck visited Loos in St. Joachimsthal (Jáchymov, Czech Republic), where Loos had been trying to procure new architectural commissions. In Rukschcio and Schachel's *Adolf Loos — Leben und Werk* it is noted that there was a question as to whose money Loos had been spending during his marriage to Claire. Was it Claire's or Otto Beck's? At first Otto demanded that Loos repay him some thirty-nine thousand crowns, which Loos did not have. Loos offered his future salary from architectural commissions, but rather than waiting for new clients to materialize, Otto responded that Loos should instead sign over his Vienna flat, presumably for Claire to continue to live there.

Adolf Opel's *Adolf Loos — Der Mensch* records that shortly following Loos' death, Elsie Altmann, Loos' second wife to whom Loos left his personal estate, recounted to Opel that Claire begged Elsie to give her the Vienna apartment. Elsie refused, and over the following few years it is apparent through Claire's letters that she lived an itinerant life. One in particular to Kurt Unger, dated June 11, 1934, indicated he should reply to her care of a school for ceramics on Würthgasse XIX in Vienna since, as she wrote, "I have no fixed address."

Beck and Schanzer family oral histories reveal that deep

connections persisted between the extended Beck family and Loos, despite temporary financial disagreements. Claire's brother-in-law, Stefan Schanzer, had helped maintain Loos' flat in Vienna for Claire and Loos, even after Loos no longer had the stamina to ascend the six flights up to his apartment starting in 1931. Receipts between Loos and Schanzer, now at the Albertina, demonstrate this support. In 1932, Schanzer is reported to have barred Franz Glück entry into the flat when he attempted to retrieve photos for a Loos monograph that he was preparing. This may have been out of a deep allegiance Schanzer felt for Otto and Claire during the divorce negotiations, however, the full reasons for this supposed action on Schanzer's part are not known. Clearly documented, however, is that subsequent to this incident Loos' loyal and long-suffering housekeeper Mitzi wrote to Loos that she was very unhappy about the Glück situation, as she was apparently powerless, not having the key to the cabinet where the photos were stored.

During Claire and Loos' divorce period, financial disagreement between the Becks and Loos may have been settled in two ways. First, Claire's divorce documents indicate that she offered to give up any alimony payments as long as Loos admitted full responsibility for the failure of the relationship. Interestingly, the legal counsel hired by her parents was Dr. Gustav Scheu, another of Loos' clients. Second, there may have been a commendation from Loos for Claire's sister Eva Schanzer and her family to buy a house in the experimental

Viennese workers housing project, the Werkbundsiedlung. Loos was a pre-visionary for this type of small-scale housing solution during his years as Chief Architect with the City of Vienna between 1920–1922; when the Werkbundsiedlung was realized in the 1930's, Loos was invited to design and build two duplexes there, which were completed with Heinrich Kulka who refined the plans and supervised the construction. Ultimately, we know the Schanzers felt that Loos' duplexes were too small in which to raise their family and so in 1932 and with the help of Otto Beck — any possible negotiations with Loos aside —, they acquired 46 Woinovichgasse, which was designed by Loos' student Jacques Groag.

Because books about Loos have not reported the later developments in Beck-Schanzer history, they will be recounted here.

The Schanzers fled their Werkbundsiedlung house shortly after Eva Beck Schanzer's apparent suicide on June 19, 1938, following the *Anschluss* (the German annexation of Austria on March 12, 1938). Eva had contracted scarlet fever, known to have been brought across the border by German soldiers, and was hospitalized. As was the practice at that time, she was quarantined behind glass, and there as Eva's husband Stefan recounted, she was threatened and psychologically tormented by anti-Semitic taunts and slurs. She became despondent. At the time of her death, roughly five thousand Austrian Jews had committed themselves to a similar fate in response to the German occupation.

Within a few weeks Stefan took his children Karl (Charles) and Doris to Pilsen to live with their grandmother Olga Beck. She took charge of her grandchildren's education during their nine-month stay as an edict had been passed barring Jewish children from attending school. Meanwhile, Stefan went to Paris on a business travel visa and attempted to arrange papers for everyone to leave Czechoslovakia.

Following many trials and tribulations to escape war torn Europe, Stefan (Steve) eventually arrived in the United States. The Werkbundsiedlung house was looked after by Claire's best friend and student of Loos, Ilse Günther (von Hennig), during the war. Steve left Europe bringing his admiration of Loos with him. When his son Charles was a teenager with an interest in architecture, Steve wrote to him in Australia from New York on March 28, 1947, "Your uncle Loos said always, [he] who wants to be a good architect should first be a good carpenter." Charles was later taken on as an apprentice with Frank Lloyd Wright, perhaps in part because he was related to Loos, whom Frank Lloyd Wright knew of and respected. Wright invited Loos to the US on several occasions including in 1933, as noted in *Adolf Loos — Leben und Werk*, for an exhibition at the Art Institute in Chicago whose theme was "organic architecture" from around the world. At this time, however, Loos' health was quickly declining and he could only write in response on February 22: "Frank Wright [sic.] is the best architect of the Americas." Sadly, Loos died six months later, on August 23, 1933, before the architects could ever meet each other.

PHOTOGRAPHS

Claire Beck Loos and Adolf Loos with the ear horn he used because of his progressive deafness. Photograph by Loos' former student, Gustav Schleicher, Stuttgart, Germany, 1931.

FAMILY ARCHIVES.

LEFT The original 1936 dust jacket for *Adolf Loos Privat* by Claire Beck Loos, with Loos portrait by photographer Hede Pollak. Claire worked in Pollak's atelier in Prague, Czechoslovakia. The book was financed by the Otto Beck family and published by the Johannes-Presse in Vienna, Austria, which was connected to Otto Nirenstein's Neue Galerie. A limited edition of 1000 copies were printed and sold to raise funds for Loos' tombstone. *FAMILY ARCHIVES.*

Im Spätherbst 1935 erscheint im Ve
der Johannes-Presse in Wien das W

ADOLF LOOS PRIVAT
VON CLAIRE LOOS

Frau Loos, die letzte Gattin des viel zu früh verstorbene[n] Meisters, erzählt in diesem Buch von den letzten Jahren seines Lebens, sie spricht von vielen seiner Arbeiten und von Menschen, die seinen Weg in dieser Zeit kreuzten. Die Form der Schilderung, die Frau Loos gewählt hat, ist überaus lebendig, es sind Momentaufnahmen von unmittelbarer Frische. Für alle Freunde und Verehrer Adolf Loos' wird dieser Band eine Fundgrube und eine Erinnerung an seine große Zeit sein. · Das Buch erscheint im Format von 12×17 cm, bei einem Umfang von zirka 160 Seiten.

Preis des Ganzleinenbandes S 5,40.

Bestellungen durch jede Buchhandlung oder direkt beim Verlag der Johannes-Presse, Wien I, Grünangergasse 1.

oder mit beiliegendem Erlagschein.

RIGHT Original publication announcement for *Adolf Loos Privat* by Claire Beck Loos from the Johannes-Presse, Vienna, autumn 1935. English translation by Claire's brother-in-law Steve Shanzer (Stefan Schanzer), circa 1950's. *FAMILY ARCHIVES.*

"Mrs. Loos, the last wife of the master who died much too early, tells in this book about the last years of his life and a great deal about his works and the people who crossed his path during this time. The form of the story Mrs. Loos chooses is very lively and contains snapshots of immediate freshness. For all his friends and admirers, this book will be a discovery and a reminiscence of this great time. The book will appear in the size of 12 x 17 cm and has about 160 pages."

Claire Beck Loos, possible self-portrait, circa late 1930's.
FAMILY ARCHIVES.

Calling card of Claire Beck circa 1920's.
FAMILY ARCHIVES.

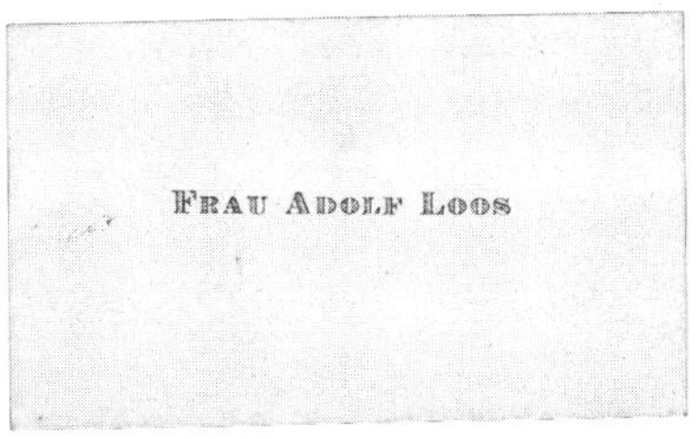

Calling card for Claire Beck Loos, circa 1929–1932. *FAMILY ARCHIVES.*

LEFT TO RIGHT Otto Beck, Max Beck, Claire Beck, Olga Beck, and Eva Beck dining lakeside in St. Gilgen, Austria, summer 1920. *FAMILY ARCHIVES.*

LEFT TO RIGHT Unidentified driver, Eva Beck (standing holding onto her hat), Olga Beck, and Claire Beck, seated on the lap of Otto Beck on a drive in their hackney carriage, Pilsen, Czechoslovakia, circa 1909. *FAMILY ARCHIVES.*

LEFT Eva Beck, Olga Beck, and Claire Beck, studio portrait by Pilsen photographer Jan Langhans (1851–1928), 1908. *FAMILY ARCHIVES.*

BELOW Postcard from Olga Beck to Otto's brother Robert Beck. LEFT TO RIGHT Max Beck, Olga Beck, Claire Beck, and Eva Beck boating in Carinthia, Austria, 1913. *FAMILY ARCHIVES.*

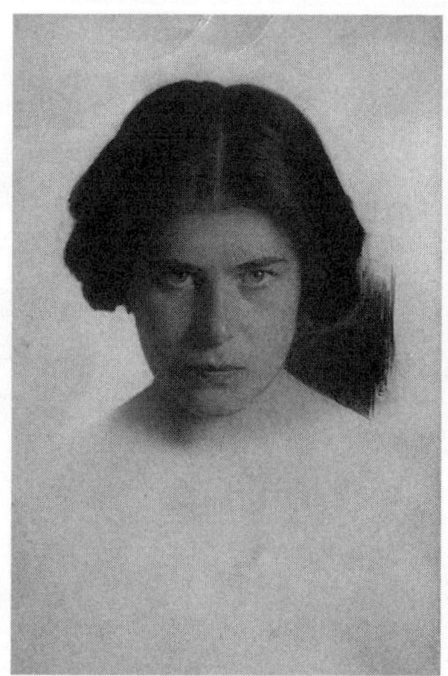

Claire Beck, studio portrait, Dresden, circa 1922. *PHOTO: GEORG RICHTER.*

ABOVE Eva Beck and Claire Beck in Austrian dress for a costume party at the Beck apartment, Klattauerstrasse 12, Pilsen, Czechoslovakia, circa 1920. Eva wears a traditional dirndl and Claire, lederhosen (leather breeches) and a hat with a feather. *FAMILY ARCHIVES.*

RIGHT Eva Beck studio portrait, circa mid-1920's. Eva, a dancer and physical therapist, was inspired by Isadora Duncan, the pioneer of modern dance. Photographer unattributed, possibly Claire Beck. *FAMILY ARCHIVES.*

RIGHT The Beck sisters, Eva and Claire, in Mozart era dress at a costume party, circa 1917.

FAMILY ARCHIVES.

BELOW Engagement party for Eva Beck and Stefan Schanzer, given by Otto Beck in the Austrian Alps at Seehotel, on Altaussee Lake, Altaussee, Styria, Austria, December 7, 1925. LEFT TO RIGHT Olga Beck, Rosa Schanzer, Baroness Elsa Felix Pollack-Parnegg, Otto Beck, Eleonore Hirsch Beck (mother of Otto Beck), Baron Felix Pollack-Parnegg (Rosa Schanzer's cousin), Eva Beck, Stefan Schanzer, Claire Beck, and Max Beck.

FAMILY ARCHIVES.

LEFT Beck family in the dining room of the first Loos-designed Beck apartment, Klattauerstrasse 12, Pilsen, Czechoslovakia, New Year's Eve 1927. LEFT TO RIGHT Eva Beck Schanzer, Stefan Schanzer, Otto Beck, Olga Beck, and Max Beck. *PHOTO: CLAIRE BECK.*

ABOVE Claire's father Otto Beck reading in the living room inglenook of the first Loos-designed apartment, Klattauerstrasse 12, Pilsen, Czechoslovakia, 1928. The Becks moved to Benešplatz 2 later in the year, another apartment designed by Loos. *PHOTO: CLAIRE BECK.*

ABOVE New Year's Eve party at the second Loos-designed Beck family apartment, Benešplatz 2, Pilsen, Czechoslovakia, December 31, 1929. LEFT TO RIGHT STANDING Mr. Günther, Karlchen Beck, Otto Beck, Mr. Weiss, Max Beck; SITTING Bruno Kleber, Mrs. Günther (behind), Trude Halm, unidentified man, Heinzi Adler, Gerti Weiss, Olga Beck (on chair), Adolf Loos, and Ilse Günther.

PHOTO: CLAIRE BECK LOOS.

LEFT Claire Beck, circa mid-1920's.

FAMILY ARCHIVES.

Claire's father Otto Beck was adamantly opposed to Loos and Claire's plans to wed. In the spring of 1929 the couple hastened toward marriage before their plans could be sabotaged. While courting Claire, Loos wrote several letters to her from Vienna that can be read as indications of the insurmountable fact of his illnesses and her family's resistance. Excerpts from his letters quoted here have been translated by Gunar Hochheiden from Rukschcio and Schachel's *Adolf Loos — Leben und Werk*.

> On April 8, 1929: "My dear Lärle, I am an old donkey and I have cried like a little child. If you cannot get the passport for me, I have no idea what to do. … I miss you very much. … Your father is right — I am a deaf cripple. I will be very grateful for every day you want to stay with me. … Yours, Dolf"
>
> April 23, 1929: "Lerle, sweety, I thank you that you have thought of me in three letters. As a good daughter of your father, I thought you had forgotten me. Today I met with your father; he is well, but he has sleepless nights because of you. I told him it would be very convenient if you became my secretary. Everything fine [sic.]. But he said you would be too good for that. You have to marry a young man. Then everything will be alright in marriage. He will find this young man, I guess. I told him, he should not think so much. 'A man who does not know where to go, will come farthest,' Cromwell the revolutionary says. I have promised him (your father) by handshake, that I will never hinder you from getting married if he finds somebody. The both of us are best friends. He is completely right about me. … I am fine, my little hero! Kisses, Dolf"
>
> July 4, 1929: "My beloved Lerle, I thank you for the nice letter, I feel sorry for you for the sorrows you are having on my behalf. … I do not feel well. I am tired, and if this feeling remains, I cannot live long anymore. I am really old. … Poor Klärle! But I console myself, either I will recover or you will become a widow soon. This cannot

Claire and Loos' wedding photo. LEFT TO RIGHT Mitzi Schnabl, Loos' housekeeper; unidentified man; Claire Beck; Adolf Loos; Heinrich Kulka, Loos' former student; and Claire's mother Olga Beck; Vienna, July 18, 1929. *FAMILY ARCHIVES.*

> last. … Why did you fall in love with me? … People should have left us alone, but they tried to separate us. Now we get married [sic.]. I hope everything will get different [sic.]. Your husband kisses you intensively."

Witnesses of Claire and Loos' marriage in Vienna on July 18, 1929 included Mitzi Schnabl, Loos' housekeeper; Claire's mother Olga Beck; and Loos' former student, Heinrich Kulka. Otto Beck refused to attend, though Loos does write to Claire that at least he will be invited for lunch.

RIGHT Adolf Loos, reading in his living room inglenook at his apartment, Giselastrasse 3 (now Bösendorferstrasse), Vienna I, circa 1929.
PHOTO: CLAIRE BECK.

ABOVE Adolf Loos' 60th birthday party, Villa Müller, Prague, Czechoslovakia, December 10, 1930. LEFT TO RIGHT STANDING architect Josef Gočár, Baron Karl Nádherný von Borutin; LEFT TO RIGHT SEATED Dr. Ing. František Müller, Claire Beck Loos, Milada Müller, Adolf Loos, Karl Kraus, Baroness Sidonie Nádherný von Borutin, Baroness Valentine Mladota-Codelli-Lumbe, Countess Maria Dobrzensky von Dobrzenicz; STANDING RIGHT-SIDE Count Dobrzensky von Dobrzenicz (?), Baron Mladota von Solopisk (?). (*Adolf Loos — Leben und Werk*, Rukschcio and Schachel, 1982).
PHOTO: STUDY AND DOKUMENTATION CENTRUM, VILLA MÜLLER, PRAGUE, CZECH REPUBLIC.

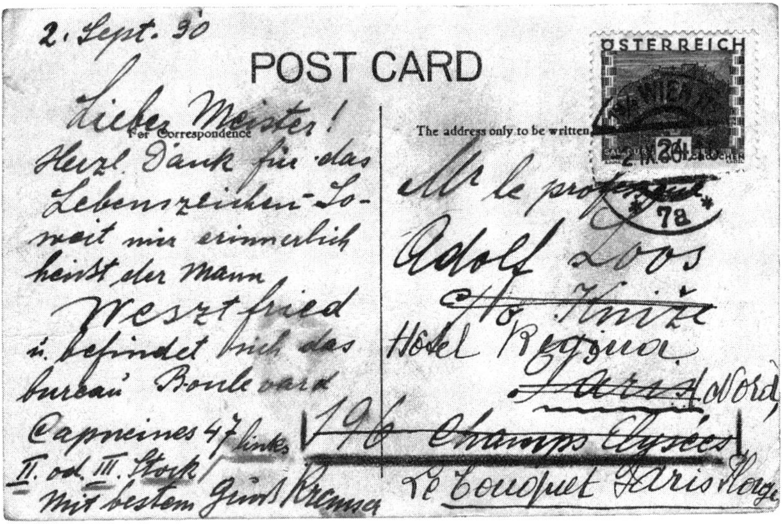

2. Sept. 30

POST CARD

Lieber Meister!

For Correspondence

Herzl. Dank für das Lebenszeichen. Soweit mir erinnerlich heisst der Mann Wesztfried u. befindet sich das bureau Boulevard Capucines 47 links II. od. III. Stock

Mit bestem Gruss Kremser

ÖSTERREICH

The address only to be written

Mr le professeur

Adolf Loos

~~c/o Knize~~

Hotel Regina

~~Paris~~ Nord

~~196 Champs Elysées~~

Le Touquet Paris Plage

ABOVE Postcard to Adolf Loos in Paris from one of his contractors in Vienna, Kremser, thought to have been a wallpaperer (Rukschcio and Schachel, 1982). The card was originally addressed c/o Loos' prestigious Viennese architectural clients, Knize Gentlemen's Outfitters. Loos completed the Knize Paris branch on Champs Elysées in 1927. The postcard may have been given by Claire to her brother-in-law Stefan Schanzer when he fled to Paris in 1938. *FAMILY ARCHIVES.*

September 2, 1930

Esteemed Sir: Sincere thanks for a sign of life. As I remember the man's name: Wesztfried. The office is located on Boulevard Capucines 47, 1st or 2nd floor.
With best greetings,

Kremser

RIGHT Claire's father Otto Beck at his desk in the living room of Benešplatz 2, Pilsen, Czechosovakia, circa early 1930's. *PHOTO: CLAIRE BECK LOOS.*

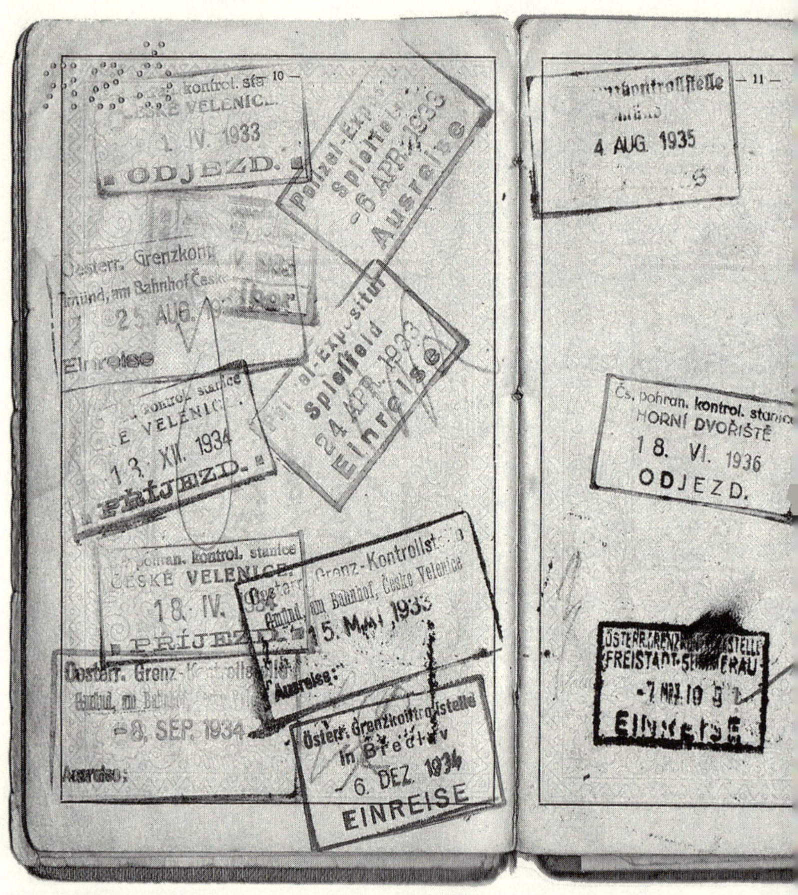

ABOVE Passport of Claire Beck Loos. A faint stamp on the left page indicates she entered Austria on August 25, 1933, possibly to attend the funeral for her former husband Adolf Loos, who died on August 23. Another page shows she went back to Czechoslovakia the same day.

FAMILY ARCHIVES.

RIGHT Olga Beck and unidentified friend admiring Olga's birthday gifts of shoes and gloves. Photograph taken in the living room of the Loos-designed apartment at Benešplatz 2, Pilsen, Czechoslovakia, June 4, 1934. LEFT TO RIGHT Otto Beck, Max Beck, family friend, and Olga Beck.

PHOTO: CLAIRE BECK LOOS.

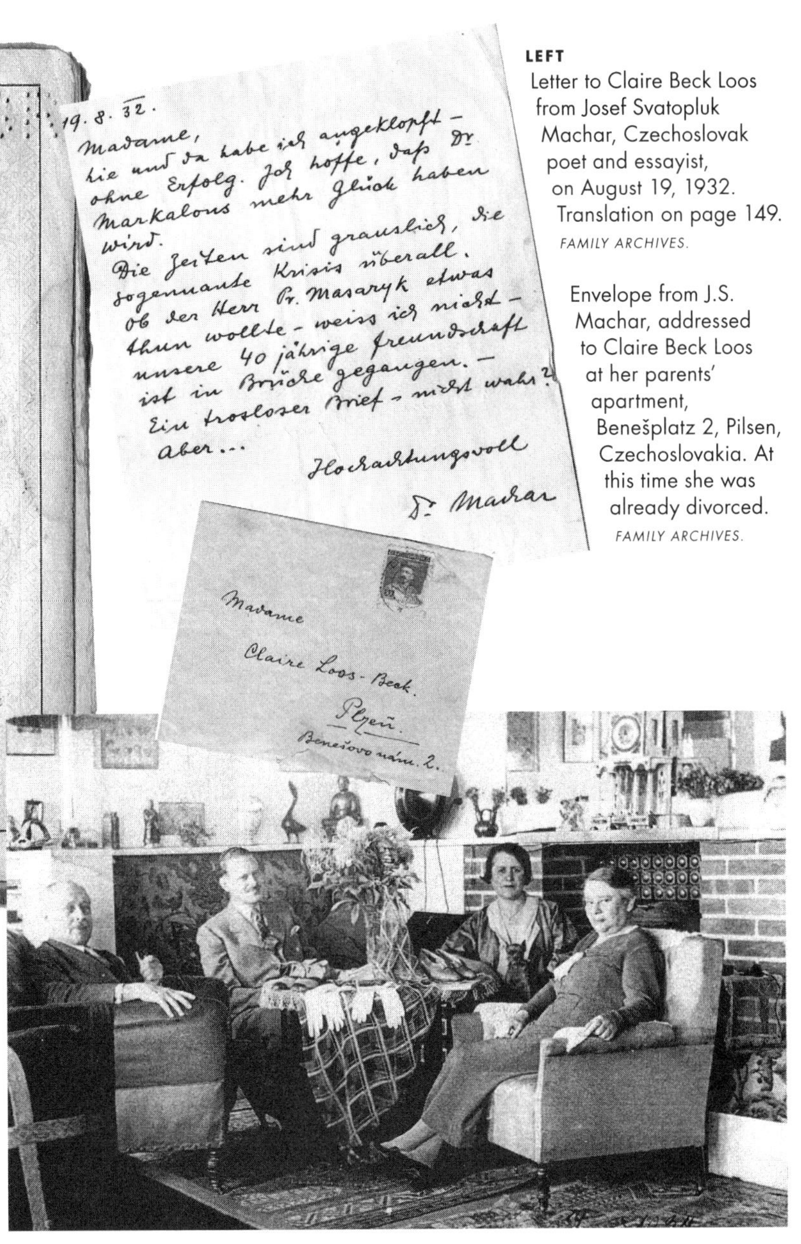

19. 8. 32.

Madame,

hie und da habe ich angeklopft – ohne Erfolg. Ich hoffe, daß Dr. Markalous mehr Glück haben wird.

Die Zeiten sind grauslich, die sogenannte Krisis überall. Ob der Herr Pr. Masaryk etwas thun wollte – weiss ich nicht – unsere 40 jährige Freundschaft ist in Brüche gegangen. – Ein trostloser Brief – nicht wahr? aber...

Hochachtungsvoll

Dr. Machar

Madame

Claire Loos-Beck.

Plzeň.

Benešovo nám. 2.

LEFT

Letter to Claire Beck Loos from Josef Svatopluk Machar, Czechoslovak poet and essayist, on August 19, 1932. Translation on page 149.

FAMILY ARCHIVES.

Envelope from J.S. Machar, addressed to Claire Beck Loos at her parents' apartment, Benešplatz 2, Pilsen, Czechoslovakia. At this time she was already divorced.

FAMILY ARCHIVES.

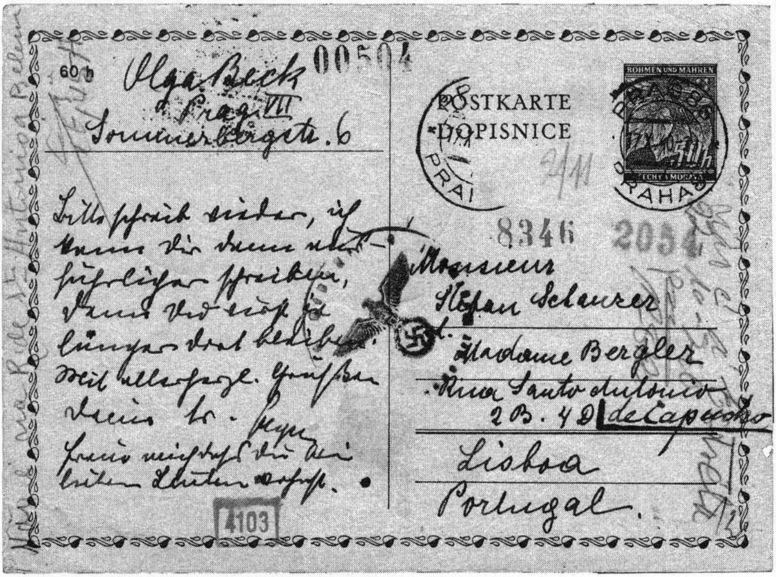

60 h

Olga Beck
Prag VII
Sommerbergstr. 6

00504

POSTKARTE
DOPISNICE

8346 2054

Monsieur
Stefan Schanzer
Madame Bergler
Rua Santo Antonio de Capucho
23. 4 D
Lisboa
Portugal.

4103

ABOVE Reverse of postcard from Olga Beck to her son-in-law Stefan Schanzer in Lisbon, Portugal following his escape on foot and by bicycle from occupied France. Postcard dated October 16, 1940.

FAMILY ARCHIVES.

Dear Stefan,
I was so happy to get your card, after waiting so long. I just knew you would make your way. Please write again; I can then write you in more detail, since you will have to be staying there longer. With warmest greetings,

Your dear Olga
I am glad you are living with nice people.

LEFT Olga Feigl Beck, mother of Claire Beck Loos. Photograph possibly by Claire, circa late 1930's.

FAMILY ARCHIVES.

RIGHT Claire's sister Eva Beck Schanzer, circa 1938. This portrait was taken by Claire, and it appears she left her thumbprint on the left side in the developing process.
PHOTO: CLAIRE BECK LOOS.

LEFT Claire's niece Doris Schanzer in the Beck apartment, Benešplatz 2, Pilsen, Czechoslovakia, 1939. Doris and her brother Karl (Charles) lived with Olga Beck after fleeing their Vienna home following the German annexation of Austria. They lived in the Beck apartment approximately nine months, before travelling alone to Paris to rejoin their father Stefan Schanzer.
PHOTO: CLAIRE BECK LOOS.

Elizabeth (Betty) Beck, Max Beck, and Martha Hirsch (widow of Wilhelm Hirsch, Otto Beck's cousin) on one of their frequent trips to see each other over the years. Paris, circa early 1950's.
FAMILY ARCHIVES.

Janet Beck Wilson on the living room settee at the Villa Müller, Prague, Czech Republic, December 10, 2006, for the annual celebration of Loos' birthday.
PHOTO: LYN COOPER

ABOVE Ilse Günther von Hennig, Steve Shanzer (Stefan Schanzer) and Max Beck, on a picnic while visiting Elizabeth (Betty) and Max Beck in Worthing, England, circa early 1970's. *PHOTO: ELIZABETH BECK.*

RIGHT Backstage after "Silenced Voices: A Terezín Memorial Concert" with works by Hans Krasa, Viktor Ullmann, Pavel Haas, and Gideon Klein performed in memory of Claire Beck Loos and her mother Olga Feigl Beck, Aspen Music Festival and School's Harris Concert Hall, Aspen, Colorado, August 6, 1995.

LEFT TO RIGHT Hawthorne String Quartet members Si-Jing Huang and Ronan Lefkowitz; Claire Beck Loos' nieces and nephew Doris Schanzer Schneider, Charles Paterson (Karl Schanzer), and Janet Beck Wilson; Mark Ludwig, Terezín Music Foundation Director, and Sato Knudsen. *PHOTO: FONDA PATERSON.*

LEFT Charles Paterson and Janet Beck Wilson, Pilsen, Czech Republic. Location of the second Beck apartment by Adolf Loos, Benesplatz 2, top floor on the left. Building façade as seen from the park, 1994.
PHOTO: FONDA PATERSON.

Einlieferungsschein Nr. 5816

Klara Loos,

Prag VII., Grüne Gasse 4.

Prag, am 11. XII. 1941

HADEGA

Handelsgesellschaft m. b. H.

Aufbewahren!

Claire Beck Loos, possible self-portrait, circa late-1930's. *FAMILY ARCHIVES.*

Last known document belonging to Claire Beck Loos, a deposit slip dated December 11, 1941, the day after Claire was assigned number 824 for transport "L" to Terezín. She was required to relinquish her remaining property to the Hadega company, for "safekeeping." Of note is Claire's address and that she kept her married name. *FAMILY ARCHIVES.*

AFTERWORD

When *Adolf Loos — A Private Portrait* by Claire Beck Loos is looked at through a historical lens, the book significantly changes. It is not only important to consider her work as literature, but also to see it as a document that reveals the *Zeitgeist* in Vienna and Czechoslovakia at the time, and gives a socio-political context to disastrous events which unfolded rapidly after the book was written.

The fact that Claire concludes her book on a heart-rending note suggests *Adolf Loos – A Private Portrait* should be considered within the tradition of German literature and cultural forms like the *Bildungsroman* or opera. After they separate and Loos refuses to take her back, she cries out, "Why is it suddenly so dark in me? / All of the lights in my soul have gone out!" Due to his brilliance, and his cruel retraction, he seems to extinguish her, but ultimately it is he who is doomed to die. Sometime in his final months, however, their mutual, ongoing love and affection breaches the gap, and stays his death. Claire leaves them together, gazes locked, the eternal moment punctuated by a final ellipsis. This mark of three dots leading into the empty white page below represents the narrator's voice as a sustained musical note that fades with the last breath.

Theatricality is embodied throughout Claire's writing, which commands vivid dialogue and leads the reader into scenes that unfold through a movement of commas, linking thoughts to images. The narrative acquires additional weight as her romance with Loos progresses, taking on a dark undertone due to their age difference and his physical frailty. It rapidly becomes clear that their love will end soon after it has begun. One can only imagine the intensity of this relationship for her, as its crushing weight and life-changing implications position her, even in her vital youth, as a tragic character. Yet she gains a personal strength through the course of the story, and objectivity about herself in relation to the world, both of which make her capable of facing Loos' mortal illness.

These themes hint at how one must engage the lessons of history to grasp the full implications of Claire's clever, bright book, which draws to a close in suspended grief. When seen through the scrim of her own untimely death, *Adolf Loos — A Private Portrait* truly has the beauty and sadness of an elegy. With book in hand, nevertheless, the reader might perform a twist of history for Claire. That she lost her specificity to a faceless grave, lost her voice and her personhood — all this can be denied every time someone reads her book, which restages and recaptures her vital presence. This volume is indeed the best place for her to be remembered, not as an echo, but a person.

In Loos' last collection of writings *Trotzdem, 1900–1930,* he wrote, "Only a very small part of architecture belongs to art: the sepulcher and the monument." Claire's immemorial art happens to be this book, a 'tomb,' and Loos' own monument. Is it architecture, in the broadest sense of the word?

Claire, who was as much a student of Loos' as all those he kept in his company, has indeed constructed, as she says in her Foreword, "a form." Her personal, imagistic, and literary stories become a cohesive, iconographic work that provide for a continual reading and a re-staging of his voice in concert with her own.

What would Loos have made of Claire's final, anonymous resting place? The entrance to the memorial at Bikernieki Forest, where Claire is presumably buried in a mass grave, and where some forty thousand other people also remain, is marked by a white monument, which has the appearance of an outlined, but broken, open-faced cube. A path under it leading into the woods opens onto a field of rough stone totems filling a pit, each different in color, weight, and texture. Like Loos' own marble walls, they embrace human form in terms of the geologic; both Loos' work and the Bikernieki memorial are nothing less than architecture meant to withstand the centuries. He famously wrote in *Trotzdem*, translated by Karsten Harries in *The Ethical Function of Architecture*, "When we find in the forest a mound, six feet long and three feet wide, raised by a shovel to form a pyramid, we turn serious and something inside us says: here someone lies buried. That is architecture" (292). Loos understood building and architecture as nothing less than a way to embrace humanity.

Claire's own life story within the larger historical context of the Holocaust is rarely reported in any books about Loos. But with this information we might begin to look at Loos' architecture in a different way — as embedded within the cultural and political movements of his time. Who were Loos' clients, and what happened to them? Some died, as did Claire and her mother Olga, at the hands of the Nazis, others like Claire's sister Eva's family, had their lives torn asunder or destroyed. Others like the Hirsches, the Semlers, and Claire's brother Max Beck luckily emigrated to Australia, England, and beyond, counting among the refugees who were absorbed into the greater global Jewish diaspora.

As more works about and by Loos become available in English, a dimension of Loos' many steps to promote an architectural approach to social integration in early twentieth century Europe can be observed. But this information is still coming to light, and critical questions about the way people lived in Loos' spaces remain unanswered. The fact that Loos was heavily engaged in a dialogue with secular Jews who were clients, friends and associates has not gone unnoticed, but it is certainly under-theorized in terms of his architecture.

It is here that the influence of secular Jewish culture, along with all the other cultures that made up the vibrant melting-pot of the Austro-Hungarian empire, need to be integrated into the story of Loos' work in order to recognize his impact on that society. Are there ways of living, thinking, and being in space that are culturally specific, and did Adolf Loos work with certain religious and cultural markers that would make his clients feel at "home"? Did these Loosian ideas of a "home" specific to the bodies that would occupy it percolate out into Loos' other more public works? What is the relationship between the personal and the public in Loos' work? *Adolf Loos — A Private Portrait* provides a small window onto what can become a multitude of questions. These have only been partially explored by other scholars, and so Claire's book may suggest alternate possibilities to begin re-reading Loos' legacy of work.

Claire makes subtle suggestions in her book about the way Loos would operate in collaboration with his clients, many of whom we know from the Beck and Hirsch family history were reform-minded, secular Jews. Loos also surrounded himself with Jewish students, and intentionally made friends with the Jewish intelligentsia — Ludwig Wittgenstein, Peter Altenberg, and Tristan Tzara, to name a few. The legacy of Jewish thought and philosophy in architecture has been taken up by several notable scholars, including historian Anthony Vidler who wrote about Freud's sense of "home" in his book *The Architectural Uncanny.* However, there is still much work to be done, and Loos, whose circle were critics of Freud, would be an important architect to contrast with the great psychoanalytic master.

As Claire intimates and illustrates, Loos was a radical who also appreciated gentility and still gravitated toward royalty and palaces. He was also an admirer of classical architecture who was yet a futurist, reforming his own culture as it struggled to change from within following the collapse of the Hapsburg monarchy and the devastation stemming from the

First World War. Loos recommended that reforms happen first at a cultural level, and that culture would then determine politics. He proposed the Viennese adjust and refine their tastes so that together they might form an "aristocracy" of the people. This new social class would glance at the same time towards both the past and the future: behind them to Vienna's glorious *fin de siècle* and forward towards a labor movement validating the craftsman and the worker. Claire quotes him, "The difference between me and a Bolshevik is only that I want to turn all the people into aristocrats, whereas he wants to turn them all into proletarians." Loos' philosophy was that people, at the very least, should live in more dignified environments.

It is already clear through many of the stories Claire relates that Loos privileged the experience of people living in his spaces over any architectural measure, in particular with regard to the Villa Müller, arguably one of Loos' most significant projects. Max Thun-Hohenstein, the *Bewegung* body movement researcher even wrote as his submission to Loos' 60th birthday book, "Loos endorses a real field-measurement *[Naturmass]. Naturmass* is a step, foot, shoe, cubit." The architect, using proportions relative to ancient measurements like the cubit — based on the length of the forearm — and the ordinary movement of a shoe, clearly used the dimensionality of the body to create space. Thun-Hohenstein continues, "Walking, standing, lying, sitting were the first objects of public consideration for Adolf Loos," the result being that Loos 'human-ized' living.

Also, significantly, Loos left the interior furnishings and their habits of use for the most part to be decided by the people who would live in his apartments and houses. He was maybe, given his disposition, surprisingly willing to accommodate his clients' belongings and tastes, so long as there were no affiliations with the Wiener Werkstätte, the Secessionists, or his rival Josef Hoffmann, as Claire reports in "The Mandl House." Many dismissed these characteristics in early scholarship about the architect, considering his interiors anachronistic. But now it is clear that Loos was a selective preservationist of culture and provided a bridge between the old and new. In a Loos house, change could occur apace with his clients' lives as the new *Zeitgeist* developed.

Still, Loos advocated a language of building that would outlast fashion. Claire notes in "One Should Not Put One's Money in the Bank" that some of Loos' clients thanked him with continued honoraria because they didn't have to remodel their flats for decades. His spaces remained modern, useful, and reflective of purpose, and above all, they were meant to encourage freedom of thought.

A closer reading of Loos' interior remodelling projects may provide a way to gauge and qualify how culture was changing from within, developing a new logic and philosophy, before the crisis of fracturing that ultimately opened Austria and Czechoslovakia to German occupation. The Austro-Hungarian and Czech lands were the vibrant cultural center of Jewish life in the 19th and early 20th centuries, and well could have been for years to come. Certainly there was a different path in history available to the people of German-speaking Europe before the Shoah, before all attempts to forcibly evacuate Jews from the lands and annihilate any traces of their lives. Those paths are grown over, but are not altogether buried and inaccessible. It is possible to start with Loos and work backward. It is important to remember that Loos' death marked the end of an era, when reforms were still thought possible, before the 1934 Civil War in Austria, the rise of the Third Reich, and the near destruction of the Jewish people.

Even though Loos' views are adamant and often seem to have been inflexible, he enjoyed and valued a diverse group of people from all classes, ethnicities and walks of life. The circle of friends Claire includes in her book at the very least attest to this — artists, writers, politicians, "young girls who were freezing on the street corners" in Montparnasse, influential businessmen, socialites and descendants of royalty, and those, like Claire, who could plainly see the man had something very different to offer the world, and wanted to be a part of it.

Claire's journeys with Loos took place during the last years of his life, when he had refined and distilled his philosophies of interiority and domestic space, and when it is most apparent how he embodied culture using furnishings and architectural form. The heavy skein of his influence within the larger

Modernist legacy continues to be woven into the lives of today; however, Claire's book also suggests that the narrative of Modernism's progress will need to be reconsidered in light of the political turmoil that occurred in and around those critical years.

Early in the 20th century, Loos and the other agents in his cultural milieu like Karl Kraus, Oskar Kokoschka, and Peter Altenberg, had already rejected the bourgeoisie, the well-to-do and the monarchists, who were often conflated with real or imaginary "Jews." Indeed, Loos' annihilation of the architectural flourishes left over from the decaying Hapsburg Empire is one of his most characteristic ideological platforms. For Loos, reforms centered on "architecture", "building", and "culture." Yet we now know these very terms have proven to be less than neutral. They mark the contestation of territory, and discursive sites where ethnic or interracial tensions are located, and acted out.

What can Loos' work materially contribute to debate about the ongoing issues in European societies still struggling with issues of assimilation and difference? Addressing Loos posthumously in his eulogy at Loos' funereal Karl Kraus said, "Your vocation … was to incorporate the world by furnishing the home, regardless of what political chaos might prevail between the two." In Kraus' view, Loos was a redeemer of culture, a healer, and yet "a man unrecognized." He ultimately saw Loos' legacy as architecture that created "inner and outer order and harmony." The home, for Loos, was to be honored like a personal habit, a choice of dress, and a private space. Loos once wrote to Claire, "I have the feeling, when [Jews in kaftans] are at home they take off the kaftan" (July 4, 1929). The ability for a home to provide cultural expression was clearly on Loos' mind, and it is exceedingly interesting that he would express this philosophy to Claire, and during their courtship no less.

Loos, one of Modernism's early progenitors, also acknowledged, validated and encoded difference into ideas about civic planning as well as individual works of architecture. Inside a home, the expression of a person; outside, architecture that created a sphere of social equality despite visible ethnic and class differences. Claire quotes him in "Everyone Should Be His Own Boss": "Rich and poor; the lower middle-class worker has his own little house just like the rich businessman ... and everyone is his own boss. That is how things should be!" Loos was ever persistent in trying to concretize such utopian ideals. However, this aspect of Loos' work was relatively unnoticed in Kraus and Claire's time. Even more pronounced was the inadvertent ignorance of what seems to have been Loos' respect for the variety of people who lived in civil society and how they lived differently, but with common needs.

True to the life of any artist, Loos' work and words have engaged over a century of debate. As Janet Stewart notes in *Fashioning Vienna: Adolf Loos' Cultural Criticism* (2000), it is clear from the disordered state of his archives, the missing documents, and what is continually coming to light, that no one yet truly knows him. It could be said that Loos is an icon, or a cipher, who represents the gaps in knowledge about the Modernist movement for which he was a forerunner. It is clear that further examination of his work is necessary to more fully understand his sources, life, inspirations, temperament, and associations.

Claire Beck Loos' version of the architect must be taken with the many others that exist. Her book provides another model of reading Loos' life and as she writes, the infectious "vitality," that informed his work. *Adolf Loos — A Private Portrait* is notably different than other books about Loos, however, in that the author inhabited and later suffered the results of his time period, an era where new ideas gestured toward the purification of culture. The book and its political, historical context can remain a warning that balances other interpretations and sheds light upon how Loos brought his uncompromising, penetrating vision to bear upon the world.

CARRIE PATERSON

CARRIE PATERSON is an artist, writer, and researcher based in Los Angeles, California. For fifteen years she has contributed essays, reviews, and critical articles to a variety of art and culture publications, as well as editing art reviews and academic essays. She has taught in the visual art department's graduate studies program at California State University, Fullerton since 2003. Her areas of focus include art and science, sculpture, critical theory, performance art, and feminism. She has an undergraduate degree in literature from Yale University and a Master of Fine Arts degree from University of California, Irvine.